COLONIAL AMERICA

INTERPRETING PRIMARY DOCUMENTS

Karin Coddon, Book Editor

Daniel Leone, President
Bonnie Szumski, Publisher
Scott Barbour, Managing Editor

**GREENHAVEN
PRESS ®**

THOMSON
™
GALE

San Diego • Detroit • New York • San Francisco • Cleveland
New Haven, Conn. • Waterville, Maine • London • Munich

LIBRARY OF CONGRESS CATALOGING-IN-PUBLICATION DATA

Colonial America / Karin Coddon, book editor.
    p. cm. — (Interpreting primary documents)
Includes bibliographical references and index.
ISBN 0-7377-1084-5 (lib. : alk. paper) — ISBN 0-7377-1083-7 (pbk. : alk. paper)
    1. United States—History—Colonial period, ca. 1600–1775—Sources.
I. Coddon, Karin. II. Series.
E188 .C697 2003
973.2—dc21   2002073858

Printed in the United States of America

CONTENTS

Chapter 2: Colonial Accounts of Native Americans

Chapter 3: The Darker Side of Colonial Life

Chapter 4: Religious Life

by the General Court on her religious beliefs. The court convicts her of heresy, and banishes her from the colony.

Chapter 5: Laws and Rules of Conduct

a godly community, prescribing piety, respect for authority, and intolerance of heretics.

FOREWORD

In a debate on the nature of the historian's task, the Canadian intellectual Michael Ignatieff wrote, "I don't think history is a lesson in patriotism. It should be a lesson in truth. And the truth is both painful and many-sided." Part of Ignatieff's point was that those who seek to understand the past should guard against letting prejudice or patriotism interfere with the truth. This point, although simple, is subtle. Everyone would agree that patriotism is no excuse for outright fabrication, and that prejudice should never induce a historian to deliberately lie or deceive. Ignatieff's concern, however, was not so much with deliberate falsification as it was with the way prejudice and patriotism can lead to selective perception, which can skew the judgment of even those who are sincere in their efforts to understand the past. The truth, especially about the how and why of historical events, is seldom simple, and those who wish to genuinely understand the past must be sensitive to its complexities.

Each of the anthologies in the Greenhaven Press Interpreting Primary Documents series strives to portray the events and attitudes of the past in all their complexity. Rather than providing a simple narrative of the events, each volume presents a variety of views on the issues and events under discussion and encourages the student to confront and examine the complexity that attends the genuine study of history.

Furthermore, instead of aiming simply to transmit information from historian to student, the series is designed to develop and train students to become historians themselves, by focusing on the interpretation of primary documents. Such documents, including newspaper articles, speeches, personal reflections, letters, diaries, memoranda, and official reports, are the raw material from which the historian refines an authentic understanding of the past. The anthology examining desegregation, for instance, includes the voices of presidents, state governors, and ordinary citizens, and draws from the *Congressional Record,* newspapers and magazines, letters, and books published at the time. The selections differ in scope and opinion as well, allowing the student to examine the issue of desegregation from a variety of perspectives. By looking frankly at the arguments offered by those in favor of racial segregation and by those opposed, for example, students can better understand those arguments, the people who advanced them, and the time in which they lived.

The structure of each book in the Interpreting Primary Documents series helps readers sharpen the critical faculties the serious study of history requires. A concise introduction outlines the era or event at hand and provides the necessary historical background. The chapters themselves begin with a preface containing a straightforward account of the events discussed and an overview of how these events can be interpreted in different ways by examining the different documents in the chapter. The selections, in turn, are chosen for their accessibility and relevance, and each is preceded by a short introduction offering historical context and a summary of the author's point of view. A set of questions to guide interpretation accompanies each article and encourages readers to examine the authors' prejudices, probe their assumptions, and compare and contrast the various perspectives offered in the chapter. Finally, a detailed timeline traces the development of key events, a comprehensive bibliography of selected secondary material guides further research, and a thorough index lets the reader quickly access relevant information.

As Ignatieff remarked, in the same debate in which he urged the historian to favor truth over blind patriotism, "History for me is the study of arguments." The Interpreting Primary Documents series is for readers eager to understand the arguments, and attitudes, that animated historical change.

INTRODUCTION

The Ordeal of Utopia: Interpreting the Colonial Experience

When modern Americans think of the first colonies and those who peopled them, images of John Smith and Pocahontas, the Plymouth pilgrims, and the witch-hunting Salem Puritans usually come to mind. Like most cultural myths about a nation's earliest days, these stories are a loose blend of fact and legend, sometimes casting the English settlers as heroic adventurers, at other times emphasizing their superstitiousness and intolerance. Examining primary documents written by actual sixteenth-, seventeenth-, and eighteenth-century persons helps modern readers understand how those in the midst of the colonial enterprise saw themselves, their environment, their communities, and their adversaries. Then as now, writing was not an objective record of facts but rather a reflection of the writer's values, beliefs, and assumptions about the world. Similarly, modern readers necessarily filter the interpretation of the past through their own historical experiences. This is not to say that all facts based on historical evidence need to be regarded as suspect; however, it is important for us to keep in mind that access to history is always partial—both incomplete and inevitably biased.

The First English Colonists in Virginia
Throughout most of the sixteenth century, England's colonial enterprise lagged behind those of its continental rivals,

especially Spain. Explorers such as Hernando de Soto, Hernán Cortés, and Ponce de León traversed the New World, establishing the first European footholds in Florida, the Caribbean, and South America. As historian Lacey Baldwin Smith observes, "England's role in the drama of discovery remained until Elizabeth's reign that of a passive but avidly interested spectator, who begrudged Spain and Portugal their good fortune but lacked the energy to challenge their monopoly."[1] The English did not make a sustained effort to establish colonies in North America until almost one hundred years after Columbus's famed 1492 expedition. Inspired by the exotic travel narratives collected by English geographer Richard Hakluyt, the mercantile spirit of the Renaissance, and the desire for personal profit as well as national glory, men like Sir Walter Raleigh and Sir Richard Grenville obtained Queen Elizabeth's authorization to found a colony that Raleigh dubbed Virginia in honor of the Virgin Queen.

The first English colony, established on Roanoke Island in 1584, was a dismal failure. When ships returned in 1590 to resupply the colonists, the entire colony had disappeared. But even before then, the initial settlers were plagued by uneasy relations with the local Powhatan Indians, the harsh climate and unfamiliar terrain, supply shortages, and disease. They were hampered as well by their own lack of practical skills suitable to their survival. Many of the first Virginia colonists were gentlemen motivated by dreams of fortune based on the mistaken assumption that the New World would prove an unmined treasure trove of precious metals. These men were poorly equipped to cope with the rigors of everyday colonial existence, and as was typical among the colonists, they treated the Native Americans with a European arrogance that ranged from patronizing curiosity to blatant exploitation and ruthlessness.

The disaster at Roanoke, combined with Raleigh's fall from the queen's favor, stymied the English colonial endeavor for over fifteen years. But James I's succession in 1604 reignited interest in English settlement of the New

World. The London Company, assembled as a group of joint-stock shareholders, received a charter from the king in 1606 to found another colony. Jamestown, christened for the king, was established a year later. Nearly a third of the 150 would-be colonists died on the voyage to Virginia. The situation for those who had weathered the arduous seaboard conditions seemed likely, during the first few years, to doom Jamestown to the same fate as its Elizabethan predecessor, Roanoke. Disease, starvation, and hostilities with the Powhatans took a grievous toll on the settlers, some of whom were said to have resorted to cannibalism during "the Starving Time," as the brutal winter of 1609–1610 came to be known. One desperate colonist was rumored to have killed and eaten his wife, prompting an enduring bit of gallows humor recorded by a fellow settler in his diary: "Now, whether she was better roasted, boiled or carbonadoed (grilled), I know not, but of such a dish as powdered (salted) wife I never heard of."[2] By the time fresh supplies of colonists and provisions arrived in the spring of 1610, almost 90 percent of Jamestown's English populace had perished.

A Turning Point for Jamestown

Perhaps the most important of the Jamestown newcomers was John Rolfe, best known for wooing and marrying the native woman Pocahontas. But it was Rolfe's decision to plant, harvest, and export tobacco in 1612 that proved pivotal to Jamestown's survival. Although Raleigh is often credited with introducing tobacco into England, Rolfe's Jamestown plantation transformed the crop into a highly marketable commodity. In colonial times, smoking tobacco was commonly believed to have health benefits, but its use soon became as fashionable as it was ostensibly therapeutic. According to historian D.M. Palliser, "By 1615 . . . tobacco shops were as common in English towns as alehouses and taverns."[3] Moreover, the establishment of viable trade between England and the colonies laid the groundwork for an important and complex relationship that would persist for nearly two hundred years. England would come to regard its colonies as a valuable supplier as well as consumer of commodities. For the colonists, successful trade meant their continued existence, but it also cemented their paradoxical position toward the homeland, which was one of economic dependence and yet relative autonomy, given the vast geographical distance between themselves and England.

Because Rolfe's lucrative crop of tobacco refined and improved the quality of the native variety smoked by the Powhatans, some historians speculate that he may have received practical advice from the chief's daughter, Matoaka, better known today by her nickname "Pocahontas," which translates loosely into "Playful One." Pocahontas has become legend for saving the life of Captain John Smith when he had been captured by her tribe and scheduled for execution. While Pocahontas's role in rescuing Smith is more myth than fact, there seems little doubt that she often served as an informal intermediary between the settlers and her tribe.[4] That Pocahontas was at one point kidnapped by the English and held for ransom indicates the erratic nature of the colony's relations with the Native Americans. During this period of captivity (1612–1613) Pocahontas converted to Christianity and met John Rolfe, with whom she fell in love. As for Rolfe, he resolved to marry Pocahontas "for the good of the plantation, the honor of our country, for the glory of God, for mine own salvation."[5] With Chief Powhatan's blessing, Rolfe and Pocahontas, now christened Rebecca, wed on April 5, 1614, inaugurating a brief respite from the ongoing hostilities between the settlers and Indians. But it was a short-lived peace. Pocahontas died while on a voyage home from England in 1617, her father, Powhatan, outliving her by only a year. He was succeeded first by his brother Opitchapan, who shortly gave way to Opechancanough, who would prove to be the colonists' fiercest Native American adversary. In response to constant English land-grabbing and resource appropriation, Opechancanough led the Jamestown Massacre of 1622, in which some four hundred settlers were killed, but its consequences for the Powhatan federation were yet more severe and long-lasting.[6] More and more colonists poured in from England, outnumbering and outgunning the indigenous people. War broke out again in 1644, during which the English managed to apprehend and execute the by-now elderly Opechancanough, but as a formidable threat, the Powhatan federation had been effectively crushed. Not reconciliation, but force, had delivered the spoils of victory to the colonists.

The First New England Colonists

If the Virginia Company was formed with chiefly entrepreneurial aims in mind, the first English settlers in New England were impelled by religious rather than profit-minded goals. Since Martin Luther's break with the Roman Catholic Church in 1517, followed by Henry VIII's establishment of the Church of England in 1529, and John Calvin's embrace of radical Protestantism, or Puritanism, in 1633, Europe had become a hotbed of religious dissent, persecution, and repression. The Reformation had dramatic effects throughout continental Europe, especially in Germany, the Netherlands, and Calvin's adopted homeland of Switzerland. But except for Scotland, which embraced religious firebrand John Knox's radical Calvinism, sixteenth-century Britain attempted to maintain an uneasy middle ground between radical reform and the theological and liturgical traditions of Rome. Henry VIII, after all, had broken with Rome not over strictly religious matters but rather over the question of supreme legal authority. His daughter Mary Tudor, who reigned in England from 1553 to 1558, sought to restore Roman Catholicism to the country; her vigorous persecution of Protestants earned her the sobriquet "Bloody Mary." But Elizabeth I, Mary's younger half sister, returned to her father's policy of moderation and conciliation (which satisfied neither Catholic counter-reformers nor Protestant extremists). King James I, who ascended to the throne in 1603, was a Scottish Protestant, but if anything, his policies were viewed as even less sympathetic to the radical reformers. In particular, James's adamant espousal of the notion of divine-right monarchy, which assumed the king's absolute authority as God's lieutenant on Earth, as James himself put it. James's position bode ill for Protestants who rejected such earthly usurpation of God's absolute power.

English Puritans—those who wanted to "purify" the Christian church—were themselves divided between those who felt the Church of England might yet be reformed through continued purgation of any remnants of Roman Catholicism, and those who sought a complete break with Anglicanism, which they deemed hopelessly "Romish" (that is, similar to Roman Catholicism). This latter group of English Puritans came to be known as Separatists, and many of them fled to the more hospitable environs of the Netherlands in 1607. The pilgrims of Plymouth who sailed to America on the *Mayflower* in 1620 were Separatists, unlike the Puritans who founded the Massachusetts Bay Colony ten years later. But they shared a common aversion to what they saw as the papist trappings of the Anglican Church.

It is too simplistic, however, to cast the first New England colonists as idealistic Puritan counterparts to their more worldly brethren in Jamestown. With a few notable exceptions, such as Roger Williams, a clergyman and founder of the Rhode Island Colony, the Puritans sought religious freedom only for the like-minded among them. They were intolerant of dissent and relentless in persecuting anyone in the community perceived as ungodly, banishing individuals who questioned their theological authority and resorting to even harsher punishments, including imprisonment, torture, and death, for non-Puritan "heretics" (such as Quakers and Roman Catholics), sexual transgressors, and perhaps most notoriously, those convicted of witchcraft. In 1629 Charles I dissolved Parliament; combined with his support for Archbishop William Laud's efforts to align the Anglican Church more closely with Roman Catholic ritual, the king's actions resulted in the flight of still more Puritans to New England. The mass emigrations slowed with the 1642 outbreak of the English civil war, during which Charles, a divine-right monarch, was executed in the name of the state in 1649. Commoner Oliver Cromwell enforced strict Puritan rule in England until his overthrow and the restoration of Charles II to the throne in 1660. Historian Lawrence Stone remarks that "the failure of the great Puritan experiment at moral regeneration from 1640 to 1660 led to the (temporary) collapse of Puritanism as a major religious and moral force in English life."[7] But in the New World, the Puritans had firmly established a stronghold in the New England colonies, their values entrenched and maintained regardless of the political circumstances in England.

From the first Puritan settlement comes a colonial myth every bit as enduring and cherished as the Pocahontas–John Smith legend: the first Thanksgiving, wherein the pilgrims and Massasoit's Wampanoag Indians share a harmonious communal feast to celebrate a successful harvest. In reality, the Puritans' relations with the Native Americans were as turbulent as those of the Jamestown settlers. Despite their rejection of the English monarchy's claim to God-ordained authority, the Puritans nurtured few doubts about the divinity of their own purpose. The pilgrims regarded the epidemic that had all but wiped out the Indians of Cape Cod before their arrival as a sign of God's blessing on their new colony. Similarly, their victories and defeats in their various conflicts with the Native Americans were seen as indications of God's pleasure or displeasure over their actions. Plymouth's long-term governor William Bradford characterizes a devastating English surprise attack on an Indian village during the Pequot War of 1636–1637 as divinely sanctioned in its very brutality:

> Those [Indians] that escaped the fire were slain with the sword; some hewed to pieces, others run through with their rapiers, so as they were quickly dispatched, and very few escaped. It was conceived they thus destroyed about 400 at this time. It was a fearful sight to see them thus frying in the fryer, and the streams of blood quenching the same, and horrible was the stink

of scent thereof; but the victory seemed a sweet sacrifice, and they gave the praise thereof to God, who had wrought so wonderfully for them, thus to enclose their enemies in their hands, and give them so speedy a victory over so proud and insulting an enemy.[8]

The invocation of God's justification for military triumphs, however bloody the cost, is, of course, not unique to the

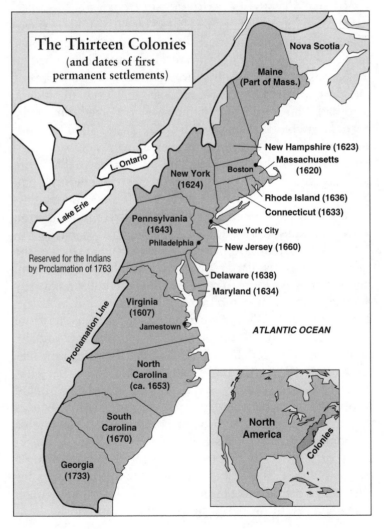

The Thirteen Colonies
(and dates of first
permanent settlements)

Nova Scotia

Maine
(Part of Mass.)

New Hampshire (1623)

Massachusetts
(1620)

Boston

New York
(1624)

L. Ontario

Lake Erie

Rhode Island (1636)

Connecticut (1633)

Pennsylvania
(1643)

New York City

Philadelphia

New Jersey (1660)

Reserved for the Indians
by Proclamation of 1763

Delaware (1638)

Maryland (1634)

Virginia
(1607)

Jamestown

ATLANTIC OCEAN

Proclamation Line

North
Carolina
(ca. 1653)

South
Carolina
(1670)

North
America

Colonies

Georgia
(1733)

Puritans. But Calvinism stressed the direct and determining divine will in all human endeavors. Calvin's "doctrine of the elect" held that God had foreordained every individual's salvation or damnation; hence, a virtuous life was no guarantee one would be spared eternal hellfire, especially when the "elect" (those predestined to be saved) were by definition few in number.

Colonial Prejudice and Persecution

Along with the general belief shared by early modern Europeans that the Indians were both "heathen" and a lesser species—a view the English had also routinely applied to the Scottish, Welsh, and Irish for centuries—the doctrine of the elect justified the Puritans' massacre even of Indians who had converted to Christianity, as occurred during the particularly bloody King Philip's War of 1675–1676. Conversely, many devout Puritans such as Massachusetts pastor Increase Mather saw King Philip's War, as well as a fire that ravaged Boston in 1676, as a sign the colonists had provoked God's just wrath for their sinfulness and increasing material prosperity. This nearly morbid preoccupation with guilt and retribution certainly seems to have contributed to an atmosphere of paranoia that fueled the Salem witch trials of 1692. Moreover, with the threat from the Native Americans to the New England colonies largely quelled, the Salem community, which consisted of Salem Town and Salem Village, seemed to seek scapegoats from within. Hundreds of Salem residents—both male and female—were charged and tried, resulting in 150 prison sentences and 19 executions. (Two dogs were also hanged.) Much of the persecutory overzealousness can be attributed to petty rivalries between Salem Town and Salem Village as well as to Puritan guilt over the community's comfortable economic status. Yet it is significant that the first person accused of witchcraft, and thus the catalyst for the ensuing hysteria, was Tituba, a black slave woman from Barbados who was a servant in the household of clergyman Samuel Parris. Superstition, excessive Puritan scrupulosity, and anxieties about the moral direction of the community mingled with racial and sexual prejudice, with infamous consequences. Only after the colony's royal governor interceded did the witch trials cease. But to this day the Salem witch hysteria remains emblematic of Puritan intolerance, moral sanctimoniousness, and superstition.

However, it is important to note that the non-Puritan mid-Atlantic and southern colonies were hardly exempt from the overall English colonialist tendency to exploit, abuse, and discriminate against those perceived as "other," whether by virtue of race, religion, or economic circumstances. That the non-Puritan colonists may have been driven by motives of material self-interest rather than religious fanaticism should not be seen as a mitigating factor in their treatment of people of color and indentured servants. Tobacco planters had a great and immediate need for cheap labor that was largely supplied through the importation of indentured servants and, beginning in 1619, African slaves. Few colonists other than Quakers (themselves a frequently persecuted minority) had any moral compunctions about either indentured servitude or slavery, despite the inhumane shipboard conditions, exploitative nature of unpaid labor, and destruction of families. Defenders of indentured servitude argued that the bondsmen (and women) were provided with food, shelter, and taught a marketable skill by which they could support themselves after their terms expired. As the last justification did not apply to slavery, perpetual bondage was justified by citation of biblical authority and appeals to the "natural" racial inferiority of nonwhites. Servitude indentures, or contracts, generally specified the bondsman receive a small parcel of land at the completion of the term (which was often as long as seven years). But the land provision soon resulted in far more new landholders than the planter class preferred. Throughout the seventeenth century slavery became increasingly the chosen source of agricultural labor in the middle and southern colonies, laying the groundwork for the sectional divisions that would eventually erupt in the American Civil War.

Law, Order, and Education

Even when focusing chiefly on the English settlers, it is difficult to generalize about the people who composed the first few generations of colonists. Those drawn to New England for primarily religious reasons tended to be older, more family-oriented, and more philosophically independent of the Crown than were the profiteers and planters of Virginia and the southern colonies. Yet from their legal documents and records of criminal proceedings, one may infer a largely conservative, even rigid dominant value system that was perhaps exacerbated by anxieties born of exposure to unfamiliar land and peoples. The colonial legal system strove to promote virtue and punish vice, deeming as sinful misconduct ranging from drunkenness and sloth to a host of sexual peccadilloes. Early marriages were the norm, although only with the approval of the proper parental, legal, and ecclesiastical authorities. Servants required their masters' permission in order to marry, and slaves were not allowed to wed at all. Children were largely regarded as their parents' property, although the parents were charged with the legal responsibility of seeing to their offspring's religious education.

This last aspect of colonial society cannot be overemphasized, for in many key ways it laid the groundwork for the notion of public education as a basic right. Because Protestantism stressed the importance of the individual's intimate relation to the word of God via the Holy Scriptures, literacy became a moral imperative.[9] While wealthy planter-class colonists had the means to import private tutors from Europe to instruct their children, the Puritans of New England viewed education not as a luxury for the privileged but as a social and spiritual necessity. In 1642 Massachusetts Bay passed laws requiring parents and masters to provide basic education to children in their care under penalty of loss of custody; Virginia enacted a similar law four years later. In 1647 Massachusetts required towns of fifty households or more to establish primary schools; larger towns (minimum one hundred households) were mandated to create secondary schools as well. By the turn of the century numerous Latin grammar schools and universities had been founded, including Harvard (1636), William and Mary (1693), and Yale (1701). Social class and gender still dictated access to education, of course; such lofty curricula as Latin, theology, and philosophy reserved for the sons of the privileged.

The Eighteenth Century: Enlightenment and Rebellion

As the threat from large-scale conflict with the Native Americans in the original colonies had greatly receded by the turn of the century, a new sense of security would shape fresh debates, divisions, and, ultimately, cataclysmic revolution for the next generation of colonists. The American colonists of the early eighteenth century faced in many ways a markedly different world from their predecessors. Benjamin Franklin, for example, was born in 1706 to a New England of bustling towns and burgeoning trade. Boston, where Franklin was born, was a flourishing seaport and the largest colonial city, with a population of twelve thousand, followed by Philadelphia and New York.[10] Visible signs suggested that the often-fanatical intolerance typical of the colonies during the previous century was ebbing: The first American synagogue was erected in New York City in 1727; five years later, the first Roman Catholic mass in the colonies took place in Philadelphia. Moreover, whereas seventeenth-century colonists were predominantly English, now new British immigrants were outnumbered by those from continental Europe seeking havens from the poverty and tyranny of their homelands. Pennsylvania and New York had become especially diverse colonies, with large populations of Dutch, Scot-Irish, and German immigrants as well as numerous French, Scandinavian, Slavic, and Mediterranean settlers.

Yet if the spirit of individualism and love of liberty brought over by the first colonists were blossoming during the early 1700s, so too were darker continuities becoming more firmly entrenched. This was especially true in the southern colonies. The Tuscarora Indian War (1711–1713) in North Carolina was a bloody reminder that the Native Americans in the original settlements were not yet completely subjugated. African slavery was also increasingly becoming the major source for the labor supply; even as Pennsylvania became the first colony, in 1712, to prohibit importing slaves to its territory, so-called Black Codes and runaway slave laws were enacted from Virginia to New York to protect the legality and perpetuity of slavery. By 1725 seventy-five thousand African slaves lived in America.

Indeed, the first half of the eighteenth century saw Puritan fervor move away from explicit persecution of dissenters toward an almost perverse emphasis on the eternal damnation awaiting all sinners (which, of course, theoretically encompassed all humanity). The revivalist movement of the 1730s and 1740s known as the Great Awakening exerted tremendous popular appeal throughout the colonies, despite or perhaps because of its theatrical focus on hellfire and its fixation on the likely doom of the individual before God. Appealing to the emotions rather than the intellect, the revivalist preachers and their sermons were accessible (and no doubt grotesquely entertaining) to the illiterate poor and the non-English-speaking immigrants. Calvinist revivalism was also theoretically democratic in its egalitarian insistence upon universal human sinfulness; although in practice, Calvinism also reinforced the idea that misfortune, poverty, and oppression were signs of inexorable damnation rather than consequences of social and political injustice and thereby potentially changeable. The so-called Protestant or Puritan ethic, deeply ingrained in American culture, was born and nurtured by the influence of Calvinism, which absolved the more fortunate from any moral responsibility to help the less privileged.

The Great Awakening was likely a counterresponse to the stirrings of the European Enlightenment, an intellectual movement that would influence many of the future American revolutionaries. The Enlightenment, embodied by the writings of Thomas Hobbes (1588–1679), John Locke (1632–1704), and Jean-Jacques Rousseau (1712–1778), among others, was in fact as diverse as Puritanism, alternately conservative and progressive, individualistic and communitarian. However, most of the Enlightenment's great philosophers shared the assumption that human beings were essentially rational and that states had a duty to govern according to the interests and "natural" rights of

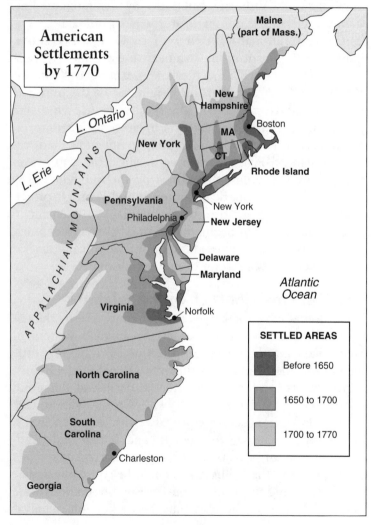

American Settlements by 1770

Maine (part of Mass.)

New Hampshire

L. Ontario

Boston

New York

MA

CT

L. Erie

Rhode Island

APPALACHIAN MOUNTAINS

Pennsylvania

Philadelphia

New York

New Jersey

Delaware

Maryland

Atlantic Ocean

Virginia

Norfolk

SETTLED AREAS

Before 1650

1650 to 1700

1700 to 1770

North Carolina

South Carolina

Charleston

Georgia

citizens. Despite the Restoration of Charles II to the throne in 1661, the English revolution had effectively dislodged the notion of absolute, divine-right monarchy as a norm of government. No longer was duty to the state necessarily seen as unilateral and nonreciprocal; rather, governments were equally bound by an unspoken contract to conform with the natural rights of subjects. This view of the state as the sum total of its citizens and not a hierarchical microcosm of God's authority embodied by the monarch, his earthly (and Anglican) surrogate, was as inimical to Enlightenment rationalists as it was to Calvinists. Indeed, many of the constitutional framers, most famously Benjamin Franklin and Thomas Jefferson, were deists who assumed that God, although the originator of the universe, played no active role in the affairs of humans, who were guided by reason and scientific principles rather than divine intervention. Although the Enlightenment exalted reason and radical Protestantism conscience, the two movements shared a common emphasis on the individual. The conjunction of pragmatic self-interest and heartfelt principle that characterizes the initial colonialist settlement in America had, by the beginning of the eighteenth century, significantly metamorphosed into a philosophically diverse but not incompatible strain of individualism.

The Growing Conflict with England

This colonial individualism was fostered as well by the relative self-sufficiency enjoyed by the English settlers of America during the seventeenth century. Britain saw little need to meddle from across the ocean in colonial administrative matters so long as its imperial needs—at this point chiefly mercantile—were met. The Crown viewed the colonies in offhandedly reciprocal terms: America was a source of raw materials for England and, in turn, a dependable consumer of British imports so long as rival merchants from Spain and the Netherlands could be constrained. The fact that, during the 1760s, non-British commodities were considered smuggled goods would play a key role in galvanizing anti-British popular dissent.

Moreover, Britain had been preoccupied militarily with its various wars with its European rivals, including King William's War (1689–1697), Queen Anne's War (1702–1713), and King George's War (1740–1748), leaving conflicts with the Indians to the colonists themselves to resolve. The absence of a centralized government in the colonies proved conducive to westward expansion, which inevitably incited more bloody skirmishes with Native Americans determined to stem the tide of conquest.

However, when Great Britain's European conflicts came to America in the form of the French and Indian Wars (1754–1763), a new era of closer government oversight and consequent colonial resistance was inaugurated. The French sought to strengthen their own colonial foothold in New France, striking up alliances with various Indian tribes to ward off English incursions along the Allegheny Mountains. As was so typically the case with the European colonial enterprise in America, at stake were mercantile interests—specifically competing claims to the Native American fur trade—as much as imperial grandeur. Although the English outnumbered the French-Indian alliance, the wars were prolonged, costly, and impeded, at least from the British perspective, by the failure of any of their Native American allies, such as the Iroquois, to abandon neutrality in the conflicts. In finally prevailing in 1763, the English may well be said to have gained what turned out to be a double-edged victory. France was left with a small remnant of its own American settlement,[11] with most of North America secured for the British, but the English victory produced the seeds of its own imperial overthrow by the colonists. The Albany Congress of 1754 proposed the first plan to unite the colonies, drawing representatives (including Franklin) from all seven, though the plan was rejected by both the colonial delegates and the British. Moreover, and even more ominously, the French and Indian Wars had driven home to the British the economic and political necessity of reining in the heretofore more or less tolerated colonial autonomy.

But it was Parliament's specific, consecutive tariff acts that galvanized the colonists, especially in the seaport colonies, where cargo ships were subject to seizure by hated royal customs officials.[12] Samuel Adams and his radical followers in the Sons of Liberty circulated anti-British pamphlets and incited mobs to defy the tariff laws by forcibly unloading cargo in Boston Harbor. In New York, customs officials were tarred and feathered by the Sons of Liberty. In Boston, lawyer James Otis raised the first of many fiery colonial voices to decry taxation without representation. Citizens affected by the duties imposed on a wide variety of staples engaged in boycotts. The significance of these boycotts has perhaps received less attention than more theatrical acts of protest, such as the Boston Tea Party. But as an effective, unspectacular form of political defiance performed by countless ordinary citizens, boycotts remain to this day integral to expressing dissent in a democratic, capitalist society.

Interpreting the American Character

The decade before the outbreak of rebellion in the colonies was so fraught with British political miscalculations that produced pivotal, crystallizing American counterreactions that historians have been tempted to cast those years in either/or terms: Either the cause of the American Revolution was taxation, hence an economic cause; or the war was fought for essentially ideological reasons, fledgling democracy struggling against the autocracy of British rule. It is true that until the imposition of the Coercive or Intolerable Acts of 1774, designed to punish Boston for the Tea Party raid, most colonists were at best lukewarm about the possibility of independence, and identified themselves as faithful subjects of the king, although not extending the same loyalty to Parliament. At the same time, however, the colonial identification with Britain was weakened by a number of factors: the vast geographical distance between America and England; the increased percentage of the population of adult citizens born in the colonies; and the fact that by

1775 fully a third of American colonists were not English in their origin. Combined with the fact that the colonists had grown accustomed to minimal interference from Great Britain prior to the French and Indian Wars, demographically most Americans were predisposed to think of themselves as separate from England.

Thus, although the fight for independence was no more a purely idealistic quest for Utopia than had been the first settlements in Virginia and Plymouth, neither was the rebellion motivated by strictly pragmatic concerns. Again, as would be the case nearly one hundred years later with the abolition of slavery, the ideological aims of so-called radicals converged historically with popular sentiment, a conjunction necessary to effect major social and political change. This conjunction between pragmatism and idealism also serves to reconcile the myths about the nation's colonial origins with the harsher facts of conquest, bloodshed, hardship, and persecution. If such a thing as an "American character" exists, it may indeed be this capacity to uphold simultaneously, sometimes paradoxically, freedom and repression, social responsibility and self-interest, tolerance and bigotry. This uniquely dual character is embodied throughout the colonial experience in the settlers' courage as well as their intolerance, their industriousness as well as their superstition, their principles as well as their dispassionate cruelties.

Notes

1. Lacey Baldwin Smith, *The Elizabethan World*. Boston: Houghton Mifflin, 1991, p. 240.
2. Quoted in Ron Thacker, ed., "Jamestown History." www.thackerworld.com.
3. D.M. Palliser, *The Age of Elizabeth, 1547–1603*. Essex, UK: Longman, 1983, p. 291.
4. Most historians regard Smith's account as somewhat unreliable. If it took place at all, the incident was more likely a ritual in which Smith's sentence and Pocahontas's intervention had been scripted.

5. Quoted in Franklin J. Jameson, *Narratives of Early Virginia.* New York: Charles Scribner's Sons, 1907, pp. 237–44.

6. The Powhatan federation was a group of around thirty tribes inhabiting the area of Virginia from Jamestown to the Potomac.

7. Lawrence Stone, *The Family, Sex, and Marriage in England, 1500–1800,* abr. ed. New York: Harper & Row, 1979, p. 176.

8. William Bradford, *Of Plymouth Plantation, 1620–1647,* ed. Samuel Eliot Morison. New York: Knopf, 1959.

9. The late–fifteenth-century invention of the printing press was itself instrumental to the development of Protestantism, as it enabled all literate Christians to have access to the vernacular Bible rather than relying on priestly interpretations of Latin scripture.

10. As of 1720, Philadelphia's population was numbered at ten thousand, and New York's at seven thousand.

11. The Treaty of Paris (1763) specified that the French cede to Britain all territory east of the Mississippi River, save New Orleans.

12. The Sugar Act of 1764 was swiftly followed by the even more incendiary Currency Act, which prohibited the colonies from printing valid paper money. The wide-ranging Stamp Act of 1765 sparked even more protest over taxation without parliamentary representation while the Quartering Act of the same year required colonists to furnish room and board to British soldiers. The Townshend Acts of 1767 affixed duties to still more imported goods, ranging from staples such as tea and paper to building materials like lead and paints. The Townshend Acts also mandated the presence of customs commissioners in Boston, which would become a pivotal underlying factor in the "massacre" of 1770.

1

COLONIZING THE NEW WORLD

CHAPTER PREFACE

Although the first English colony in the New World was not established until nearly one hundred years after Columbus's famed 1492 voyage, as early as 1496 King Henry VII authorized an Italian-born explorer, John Cabot (or Giovanni Caboto) to lead a westward expedition. It is important to remember that the chief aim of these early voyages was not to discover new lands but rather to find a western route (which was presumed to be shorter) to Asia and all of its riches. When Cabot and his crew of eighteen reached land in June 1497, they believed they had arrived in northeastern Asia. In truth, the expedition had discovered the coasts of areas known today as Labrador, Newfoundland, and New England. Cabot claimed the territory in the name of the king and sailed back to England to report his findings. King Henry VII was encouraged enough to reward Cabot with a pension that enabled a subsequent expedition in 1498, which most historians believe resulted in the loss at sea of Cabot and four or five ships carrying around three hundred men.

After lying dormant for roughly ninety years, England's exploratory impulses were revived during the mid-1580s under Queen Elizabeth I. Elizabeth's usual way of rewarding her favorite courtiers was to grant patents and monopolies, which cost the Crown itself nothing. Aside from competition with Portugal and archrival Spain, which had already founded colonies in the Western Hemisphere, the Elizabethan system of patronage and rewards encouraged the ambitions of courtiers such as Sir Walter Raleigh, then the queen's favorite courtier. In many ways the epitome of the Renaissance man, Raleigh was a soldier, scholar, courtier, and adventurer who first voyaged to Virginia in 1584. He secured Elizabeth's authorization to found the first English colony on Roanoke Island.

The colony was a spectacular failure, but the fate of Roanoke did not daunt the English for long in their quest to establish a foothold in the New World. Under James I, who succeeded Elizabeth in 1603, the London Company was formed for even more expressly entrepreneurial purposes than had been Raleigh's group. The Crown exhorted the company to seek gold and other precious metals (converting Native Americans to Christianity was of secondary importance). Not gold, however, but tobacco proved to be the source of economic sustenance and profit in the colony, encouraging many more Englishmen to try their fortunes as planters in Virginia and creating a need for inexpensive manual labor that would foster the systems of indentured servitude and slavery in the New World.

Not all of the first English colonies were founded specifically by profiteers and adventurers. Increasingly polarized religious dissent in England between Puritan separatists and Anglicans also drove seventeenth-century emigration. In 1620 the pilgrims of Plymouth arrived in what would become Massachusetts by way of the Netherlands, where they had first sought environs congenial to their religious views. Led by William Bradford, the pilgrims endured a first year nearly as brutal as the Jamestown colonists had suffered, but the peace treaty they struck with Chief Massasoit and the Wampanoag Indians enabled a period of short-lived harmony in Plymouth embodied by the harvest feast, now known as the Thanksgiving celebration.

Although the seventeenth-century colonial enterprises were fraught by hardships (many self-induced by exploitation of the Native Americans and their resources), their pursuit, respectively, of entrepreneurial and philosophical individualism inspired the first English settlers of the New World.

The Failed Colony at Roanoke

Ralph Lane

England's fierce rivalry with Spain, and to a lesser extent, with Portugal, whet the appetites of many British adventurers to establish their own foothold in the New World. Sir Walter Raleigh, the queen's favorite until displaced in the 1590s by the younger, more impetuous earl of Essex, obtained from Elizabeth a charter previously held by Raleigh's half-brother Sir Humphrey Gilbert. After claiming St. Johns, Newfoundland, for England in 1583, Gilbert had ended up drowning on the return voyage. The next year Raleigh dispatched two ships captained by Philip Amadas and Arthur Barlowe to the New World.

On July 13, 1584, Amadas and Barlowe reached the North Carolina coast, which they claimed in Elizabeth's name for Raleigh. They traveled on to Roanoke Island, where they found the land fertile and virtually idyllic, and the natives just as hospitable. They even brought back to England two Indians, Wanchese and Manteo, to attest to the geniality of the indigenous people and instruct the English about their people. Heartened, Raleigh proceeded with the plan to establish the first English colony in the land now christened "Virginia" in the queen's honor.

Seven ships led by Raleigh's cousin Sir Richard Grenville, embarked from Plymouth, England, on April 9, 1585. Among the 108 men aboard were tradesmen and gentlemen, navigators and soldiers, and Wanchese and Manteo, who had learned to speak English. Also aboard were the men who would be Roanoke's first two governors, Ralph Lane and John White. Shortly after establishing a colony

Excerpted from "The Colony at Roanoke," by Ralph Lane, *Principle Navigations, Voyages of the English Nation, III*, edited by Richard Hakluyt (London, 1600).

on Roanoke Island in the summer of 1585, Grenville left for England to secure more supplies, and Ralph Lane, appointed governor, oversaw the settlement. The colonists built a fort and small dwellings for themselves, surveyed the geography, and managed to alternately cooperate with and antagonize the natives.

The first colony lasted only ten months. Grenville's return with supplies was delayed; increasing hostility with the Indians (largely due to the colonists' actions such as burning a village and taking Indians hostage) made it all but impossible for the settlers to rely on their Indian hosts for sustenance. When Sir Francis Drake's fleet appeared off the Roanoke coast, the original colonists, in desperate need of supplies, were persuaded by Drake to sail back to England, despite Governor Lane's initial reluctance to abandon the settlement.

The following selection, from a report Lane wrote to Raleigh in 1600 (later published by Richard Hakluyt), attests to the circumstances that caused the settlers to ultimately abandon Roanoke in 1586. Lane describes their search for supplies, uneasy relations with the Indians, and the timely arrival of Drake's fleet and the captain's offer first of provisions, then of passage home to the colonists.

As you read, consider the following questions:
1. Consider the apparent tension between Lane's praise of King Menatonon and his casual reference to holding Indians hostage. How might you account for this seeming contradiction in Lane's perspective?
2. What can you infer, from this passage, were the English colonists' chief goals in settling the Roanoke colony? What do you think Lane and the settlers (and by extension, Raleigh and Grenville) hope to achieve through successful colonization?
3. What is suggested about Lane and the colonists by their initial reluctance to accept Drake's offer to return them to England? Given that this account was written after the return home, are there any indications in the text that Lane

regrets the decision, or that he is concerned about how others might regard their abandonment of the colony?

To the Northwest the farthest place of our discovery was to Chawanook distant from Roanoak about 130 miles. Our passage thither lies through a broad sound, but all fresh water, and the channel of a great depth, navigable for good shipping, but out of the channel full of shoals. . . .

Chawanook itself is the greatest province and Seigniory [dominion] lying upon that river, and that the town itself is able to put 700 fighting men into the field, besides the force of the province itself.

The king of the said province is called Menatonon, a man impotent in his limbs, but otherwise for a savage, a very grave and wise man, and of a very singular good discourse in matters concerning the state, not only of his own country, and the disposition of his own men, but also of his neighbors round about him as well far as near, and of the commodities that each country yields.

What the Explorers Learn from King Menatonon

When I had him prisoner with me, for two days that we were together, he gave me more understanding and light of the country than I had received by all the searches and savages that before I or any of my company had had conference with: it was in March last past 1586. Among other things he told me, that going three days' journey in a canoe up his river of Chawanook, and then descending to the land, you are within four days' journey to pass over land Northeast to a certain king's country, whose province lies upon the Sea, but his place of greatest strength is an island situated, as he described unto me, in a bay, the water round about the island very deep.

Out of this bay he signified unto me, that this King had so great quantity of pearls, and does so ordinarily take the same, as that not only his own skins that he wears, and the better sort of his gentlemen and followers are full set with the said pearls, but also his beds, and houses are garnished with them, and that he has such quantity of them, that it is a wonder to see. . . .

The king of Chawanook promised to give me guides to go overland into that king's country whensoever I would: but he advised me to take good store of men with me, and good store of victual, for he said, that king would be loath to suffer any strangers to enter into his country, and especially to meddle with the fishing for any pearls there, and that he was able to make a great many of men in to the field, which he said would fight very well. . . .

And for that not only Menatonon, but also the savages of Moratoc themselves do report strange things of the head of that river, it is thirty days, as some of them say, and some say forty days' voyage to the head thereof, which head they say springs out of a main rock in that abundance, that forthwith it makes a most violent stream: and further, that this huge rock stands so near unto a Sea, that many times in storms (the wind coming outwardly from the sea) the waves thereof are beaten into the said fresh stream, so that the fresh water for a certain space, grows salt and brackish: I took a resolution with myself, having dismissed Menatonon upon a ransom agreed for, and sent his son into the pinnace to Roanoak, to enter presently so far into that river with two double whirries, and forty persons one or other, as I could have victual to carry us, until we could meet with more either of the Moraroks, or of the Mangoaks, which is another kind of savages, dwelling more to the westward of the said river: but the hope of recovering more victual from the savages made me and my company as narrowly to escape starving in that discovery before our return, as ever men did, that missed the same. . . .

The Copper Mine

And that which made me most desirous to have some doings with the Mangoaks either in friendship or otherwise to have had one or two of them prisoners, was, for that it is a thing most notorious to all the country, that there is a province to the which the said Mangoaks have resource and traffic up that river of Moratoc, which has a marvelous and most strange mineral. This mine is so notorious among them, as not only to the savages dwelling up the said river, and also to the savages of Chawanook, and all them to the westward, but also to all them of the main: the country's name is of fame, and is called Chaunis Temoatan.

The mineral they say is Wassador, which is copper, but they call by the name of Wassador every metal whatsoever: they say it is of the color of our copper, but our copper is better than theirs: and the reason is for that it is redder and harder, whereas that of Chaunis Temoatan is very soft, and pale: they say that they take the said metal out of a river that falls very swift from high rocks and hills, and they take it in shallow water: the manner is this.

They take a great bowl by their description as great as one of our targets, and wrap a skin over the hollow part thereof, leaving one part open to receive in the mineral: that done, they watch the coming down of the current, and the change of the color of the water, and then suddenly chop down the said bowl with the skin, and receive into the same as much ore as will come in, which is ever as much as their bowl will hold, which presently they cast into a fire, and forthwith it melts, and does yield in five parts at the first melting, two parts of metal for three parts of ore.

Of this metal the Mangoaks have so great store, by report of all the savages adjoining, that they beautify their houses with great plates of the same: and this to be true, I received by report of all the country, and particularly by young Skiko, the King of Chawanook's son of my prisoner, who also himself had been prisoner with the Mangoaks, and set down all the particulars to me before mentioned: but he had not been at Chaunis Temoatan himself: for he said it was twenty days' journey overland from the Mangoaks, to the said mineral country, and that they passed through certain other territories between them and the Mangoaks, before they came to the said country.

Upon report of the premises, which I was very inquisitive in all places where I came to take very particular information of by all the savages that dwelt towards these parts, and especially of Menatonon himself, who in everything did very particularly inform me, and promised me guides of his own men, who should pass over with me, even to the said country of Chaunis Temoatan, for overland from Chawanook to the Mangoaks is but one day's journey from sun rising to sun setting, whereas by water it is seven days with the soonest: These things, I say, made me very desirous by all means possible to recover the Mangoaks, and to get some of that their copper for an assay, and therefore I willingly yielded to their resolution: But it fell out very contrary to all expectation, and likelihood: for after two days' travel, and our whole victual spent, lying on shore all night, we could never see man, only fires we might perceive made along the shore where we were to pass, and up into the country, until the very last day.

The Threat of Hostile Indians

In the evening whereof, about three of the clock we heard certain savages call as we thought, Manteo, who was also at that time with me in the boat, whereof we all being very glad, hoping of some friendly conference with them, and making him to answer them, they presently began a song, as we thought, in token of our welcome to them: but Manteo presently betook him to his piece, and told me that they meant to fight with us: which word was not so soon spoken by him, and the light horseman ready to put to shore, but there lighted a volley of their arrows among them in the boat, but did no hurt to any man. . . .

Choosing a convenient ground in safety to lodge in for the night, making a strong corps of guard, and putting out good sentinels, I determined the next morning before the rising of the sun to be going back again, if possibly we might recover the mouth of the river, into the broad sound, which at my first motion I found my whole company ready to assent unto: for they were now come to their dog's porridge, that they had bespoken for themselves if that befell them which did, and I before did mistrust we should hardly escape.

The end was, we came the next day by night to the river's mouth within four or five miles of the same, having rowed in one day down the current, much as in four days we had done against the same: we lodged upon an island, where we had nothing in the world to eat but pottage of sassafras leaves, the like whereof for a meat was never used before as I think. The broad sound we had to pass the next day all fresh and fasting: that day the wind blew so strongly and the billow so great, that there was no possibility of passage without sinking of our boats. This was upon Easter eve, which was fasted very truly. Upon Easter day in the morning the wind coming very calm, we entered the sound, and by four of the clock we were at Chipanum, whence all the savages that we had left there were left, but their wares did yield us some fish, as God was pleased not utterly to suffer us to be lost: for some of our company of the light horsemen were far spent. The next morning we arrived at our home Roanoak. . . .

This fell out the first of June 1586, and the eight of the same came advertisement to me from captain Stafford, ly-

According to Governor Lane, as the English tried to come ashore they were met with a volley of arrows from the Roanoke Indians.

ing at my lord Admiral's Island, that he had discovered a great fleet of three and twenty sails: but whether they were friends or foes, he could not yet discern. He advised me to stand upon as good guard as I could.

The ninth of the said month he himself came unto me, having that night before, and that same day traveled by land twenty miles: and I must truly report of him from the first to the last; he was the gentleman that never spared labor or peril either by land or water, fair weather or foul, to perform any service committed unto him.

He brought me a letter from the General Sir Francis Drake, with a most bountiful and honorable offer for the supply of our necessities to the performance of the action we were entered into; and that not only of victuals, munition, and clothing, but also of barks, pinnaces, and boats; they also by him to be victualed, manned and furnished to my contentation.

The tenth day he arrived in the road of our bad harbor: and coming there to an anchor, the eleventh day I came to him, whom I found in deeds most honorably to perform that which in writing and message he had most courteously offered, he having aforehand propounded the matter to all the captains of his fleet, and got their liking and consent thereto.

With such thanks unto him and his captains for his care both of us and of our action, not as the matter deserved, but as I could both for my company and myself, I (being aforehand prepared what I would desire) craved at his hands that it would please him to take with him into England a number of weak and unfit men for any good action, which I would deliver to him; and in place of them to supply me of his company with oar-men, artificers, and others.

That he would leave us so much shipping and victual, as about August then next following would carry me and all my company into England, when we had discovered somewhat, that for lack of needful provision in time left with us as yet remained undone.

That it would please him withal to leave some sufficient Masters not only to carry us into England, when time should be, but also to search the coast for some better harbor, if there were any, and especially to help us to some small boats and oar-men. . . .

While these things were in hand, the provision aforesaid being brought, and in bringing aboard, my said masters being also gone aboard, my said barks having accepted of their charge, and my own officers, with others in like sort of my company with them (all which was dispatched by the said general the 12 of the said month) the 13 of the same there arose such an unwonted storm, and continued four days. . . .

This storm having continued from the 13 to the 16 of the month, and thus my bark put away as aforesaid, the general coming ashore made a new proffer unto me; which was a ship of 170 tons, called the bark Bonner, with a sufficient master and guide to tarry with me the time appointed, and victualed sufficiently to carry me and my company into England, with all provisions as before: but he told me that he would not for anything undertake to have her brought into our harbor, and therefore he was to leave her in the road, and to leave the care of the rest unto myself, and advised me to consider with my company of our case, and to deliver presently unto him in writing what I would require him to do for us; which being within his power, he did assure me as well for his captains as for himself, should be most willingly performed.

Hereupon calling such captains and gentlemen of my company as then were at hand, who were all as privy as myself to the general's offer; their whole request was to me, that considering the case that we stood in, the weakness of our company, the small number of the same, the carrying away of our first appointed bark, with those two special masters, with our principal provisions in the same, by the very hand of God as it seemed, stretched out to take us from thence; considering also, that his second offer, though most honorable of his part, yet of ours not to be taken, insomuch as there was no possibility for her with any safety to be brought into the harbor: seeing furthermore, our hope for supply with Sir Richard Grenville, so undoubtedly promised us before Easter, not yet come, neither then likely to come this year, considering the doings in England for Flanders, and also for America, that therefore I would resolve myself with my company to go into England in that fleet, and accordingly to make request to the general in all our names, that he would be pleased to give us present passage with him. . . .

From whence the general in the name of the Almighty, weighing his anchors (having bestowed us among his fleet) for the relief of whom he had in that storm sustained more peril of wreck than in all his former most honorable actions against the Spaniards, with praises unto God for all, set sail the nineteenth of June 1596, and arrived in Portsmouth the seven and twentieth of July the same year.

Return to Roanoke

John White

The colony of Roanoke seems from the very beginning to have been an ill-fated enterprise. When the second group of colonists (funded again by Raleigh) reached Roanoke in 1587, they discovered only the bones of the fifteen men left behind by Grenville a year before, presumably killed by hostile Indians. The second set of colonists numbered 150, and included planters, their wives, and children. The new governor John White appointed Manteo (the Croatoan Indian who had befriended the original settlers) "Lord of Roanoke," and trusting all was well, set sail in late August 1587 for England, intending to return shortly with more supplies. Among those he left behind was his granddaughter Virginia Dare, the first English child born in America.

White's return, however, was delayed by the eruption of war between England and Spain, which required not only the attention of Raleigh and Grenville but their fleet in battling the Spanish Armada. It wasn't until 1590 that White and his men finally returned to Virginia. They found the ransacked settlement abandoned, with no sign of the colonists other than an enigmatic carving on a tree. White's discovery of the empty and ruined colony is the subject of the following selection, which originally appeared in Richard Hakluyt's *Principle Navigations*, a vastly popular collection of travel narratives published in London between 1598 and 1600.

The disappearance of the Roanoke colonists spawned a variety of theories that persist to this day. Some believe they migrated to the southern Chesapeake area, where they were killed by the hostile Powhatan Indians. Others postulate that perhaps the colonists split up, some slaughtered by

Excerpted from "Return to Roanoke," by John White, *Principle Navigations, Voyages of the English Nation, III*, edited by Richard Hakluyt (London, 1600).

the Indians and others going off to Croatoan Island with Manteo, where they intermarried with the native people. It has also been suggested that the colonists were wiped out either by drought or by an epidemic such as smallpox, with the Indians destroying the human remains to stop the disease from spreading. However, no single comprehensive theory has yet adequately explained the colonists' mysterious disappearance.

As you read, consider the following questions:
1. On what evidence does White base his belief that the colonists are still alive? Do you find such evidence credible?
2. Imagine you are a member of White's expedition. What conclusions would you draw about the fate of the colonists? Be sure to address the matter of the missing boats, the possible role of Manteo, and, of course, the carvings on the trees.
3. Should the settlers have foreseen the disaster that befell the Roanoke colony? Compare with "Instructions for the Jamestown Colony." What events or mishaps did the colonists perhaps fail to prepare for?

The 15 of August towards evening we came to an anchor at Hatorask, in 36 degr. and one third, in five fathom water, three leagues from the shore. At our first coming to anchor on this shore we saw a great smoke rise in the Isle [of] Roanoke near the place where I left our colony in the Year 1587, which smoke put us in good hope that some of the colony were there expecting my return out of England.

The 16 and next morning our 2 boats went a shore, & Captain [Abraham] Cooke, & Captain [Edward] Spicer, & their company with me, with intent to pass to the place at Roanoke where our countrymen were left. At our putting from the ship we commanded our master gunner to make ready 2 minions and a Falcon [ordnance] well loden [loaded], and to shoot them off with reasonable space between every shot, to the ended that their reports might be heard to the place where we hoped to find some of our people. This was accordingly performed, & our two boats put off unto the shore, in the Admiral's boat we sounded all the way and found from our ship until we came within a mile of the shore nine, eight, and seven fathom: but before we were half way between our ships and the shore we saw another great smoke to the southwest of Kindrikers mounts: we therefore thought good to go to that second smoke first: but it was much further from the harbor where we landed, then we supposed it to be, so that we were very sore tired before we came to the smoke. But that which grieved us more was that when we came to the smoke, we found no man nor sign that any had been there lately, nor yet any fresh water in all this way to drink. Being thus wearied with this journey we returned to the harbor where we left our boats, who in our absence had brought their cask a shore for fresh water, so we deferred our going to Roanoke until the next morning, and caused some of those sailors to dig in those sandy hills for fresh water whereof we found very sufficient. That night we returned aboard with our boats and our whole company in safety.

Dangerous Waters

The next morning being the 17 of August, our boats and company were prepared again to go up to Roanoke, but Captain Spicer had then sent his boat ashore for fresh water, by means whereof it was ten of the clock aforenoon before we put from our ships which were then come to an anchor within two miles of the shore. The Admiral's boat was half way toward the shore, when Captain Spicer put off from his ship. The Admiral's boat first passed the breach, but not without some danger of sinking, for we had a sea brake into our boat which filled us half full of water, but by the will of God and careful steerage of Captain Cooke we came safe ashore, saving only that our furniture, victuals match and powder were much wet and spoiled. For at this time the wind blue at northeast and direct into the harbor so great a gale, that the Sea broke extremely on the bar, and the tide went very forcibly at the entrance. By that time our Admiral's boat was hauled ashore, and most of our things taken out to dry, Captain Spicer came to the entrance of the breach with his mast standing up, and was half passed over, but by the rash and indiscreet steerage of Ralph Skinner his Master's mate, a very dangerous sea brake into their boat and overset them quite, the men kept the boat some in it, and some hanging on it, but the next sea set the boat on ground, where it beat so, that some of them were forced to let go their hold, hoping to wade ashore, but the sea still beat them down, so that they could neither stand nor swim, and the boat twice or thrice was turned the keel upward; whereon Captain Spicer and Skinner hung until they sunk, & seen no more. But four that could swim a little kept themselves in deeper water and were saved by Captain Cooke's means, who so soon as he saw their oversetting, stripped himself, and four other that could swim very well, & with all haste possible rowed unto them, & saved four. They were 11 in all, & 7 of the chiefest were drowned, whose names were Edward Spicer, Ralph Skinner, Edward Kelley, Thomas Bevis, Hance the Surgeon, Edward Kelborne, Robert Coleman.

Another Attempt to Reach the Colony

This mischance did so much discomfort the sailors, that they were all of one mind not to go any further to seek the planters. But in the end by the commandment & persuasion of me and Captain Cooke, they prepared the boats: and seeing the captain and me so resolute, they seemed much more willing. Our boats and all things fitted again, we put off from Hatorask, being the number of 19 persons in both boats: but before we could get to the place, where our planters were left, it was so exceeding dark, that we overshot the place a quarter of a mile: there we espied towards the north end of the island the light of a great fire through the woods, to the which we presently rowed: when we came right over against it, we let fall our grapnel [a small anchor] near the shore, & sounded with a trumpet a call, & after-

These English colonists are welcomed by Indians on the Charles River. However, not all relations with the Indians were friendly.

wards many familiar English tunes of songs, and called to them friendly; but we had no answer, we therefore landed at day-break, and coming to the fire, we found the grass & sundry rotten trees burning about the place.

The Abandoned Colony

From hence we went through the woods to that part of the Island directly over against Dasamongwepeuk, & from thence we returned by the waterside, round about the north point of the Island, until we came to the place where I left our colony in the year 1586. In all this way we saw in the sand the print of the savages' feet of 2 or 3 sorts trodden at night, and as we entered up the sandy bank upon a tree, in the very brow thereof were curiously carved these faire Roman letters C R O: which letters presently we knew to signify the place, where I should find the planters seated, according to a secret token agreed upon between them & me at my last departure from them, which was, that in any ways they should not fail to write or carve on the trees or posts of the doors the name of the place where they should be seated; for at my coming away they were prepared to remove from Roanoke 50 miles into the main. Therefore at my departure from them in Anno 1587 I willed them, that if they should happen to be distressed in any of those places, that then they should carve over the letters or name, a cross in this form, but we found no such sign of distress. And having well considered of this, we passed toward the place where they were left in sundry houses, but we found the houses taken down, and the place very strongly enclosed with a high palisade of great trees, with curtains and flankers very fort-like, and one of the chief trees or posts at the right side of the entrance had the bark taken off, and 5 foot from the ground in fair capital letters was graven CROATOAN without any cross or sign of distress; this done, we entered into the palisade, where we found many bars of iron, two pigges of lead, four iron fowlers, iron sacker-shot, and such like heavy things, thrown here and there, almost overgrown with grass and weeds. From thence we went along by the water side, towards the point of the creek to see if we could find any of their boats or pinnaces [small boats propelled by oars or sails], but we could perceive no sign of them, nor any of the last Falcons and small ordinance which were left with them, at my departure from them.

More Signs of Trouble

At our return from the creek, some of our Sailors meeting us, told us that they had found where diverse chests had been hidden, and long sithence [since] dug up again and broken up, and much of the goods in them spoiled and scattered about, but nothing left, of such things as the savages knew any use of, undefaced. Presently Captain Cooke and I went to the place, which was in the end of an old trench, made two years past by Captain Amadas: where we found five chests, that had been carefully hidden of the planters, and of the same chests three were my own, and about the place many of my things spoiled and broken, and my books torn from the covers, the frames of some of my pictures and maps rotten and spoiled with rain, and my armor almost eaten through with rust; this could be no other but the deed of the savages our enemies at Dasamong-wepeuk, who had watched the departure of our men to Croatoan; and as soon as they were departed, dug up every place where they suspected any thing to be buried: but although it much grieved me to see such spoil of my goods, yet on the other side I greatly joyed that I had safely found a certain token of their safe being at Croatoan, which is the place where Manteo was born, and the savages of the island our friends.

When we had seen in this place so much as we could, we returned to our boats, and departed from the shore towards our ships, with as much speed as we could: For the weather began to overcast, and very likely that a foul and stormy night would ensue. Therefore the same evening with much danger and labor, we got our selves aboard, by which time the wind and seas were so greatly risen, that we doubted our cables and anchors would scarcely hold until morning; wherefore the captain caused the boat to be manned with five lusty men, who could swim all well, and sent them to the little island on the right hand of the harbor, to bring aboard six of our men, who had filled our cask with fresh water: the boat the same night returned aboard with our men, but all our cask ready filled they left behind, impossible to be had aboard without danger of casting away both men and boats; for this night proved very stormy and foul.

Misfortune Hinders the Search
The next morning it was agreed by the captain and my self, with the master and others, to weigh anchor, and go for the place at Croatoan, where our planters were: for that then the wind was good for that place, and also to leave that cask with fresh water on shore in the island until our return. So then they brought the cable to the capstan [a shipboard drum used to move cables or heavy weights], but when the anchor was almost apeck, the cable broke, by means whereof we lost another anchor, wherewith we

drove so fast into the shore, that we were forced to let fall a third anchor; which came so fast home that the ship was almost aground by Kenricks mounts: so that we were forced to let slip the cable end for end. And if it had not chanced that we had fallen into a channel of deeper water, closer by the shore then we accompted of, we could never have gone clear of the point that lyeth to the southwards of Kenricks mounts. Being thus clear of some dangers, and gotten into deeper waters, but not without some loss; for we had but one cable and anchor left us of four, and the weather grew to be fouler and fouler; our victuals scarce, and our cask and fresh water lost: it was therefore determined that we should go for Saint John or some other island to the southward for fresh water. And it was further purposed, that if we could any ways supply our wants of victuals and other necessaries, either at Hispaniola, Saint John, or Trinidad, that then we should continue in the Indies all the Winter following, with hope to make 2 rich voyages of one, and at our return to visit our countrymen at Virginia. The captain and the whole company in the Admiral (with my earnest petitions) thereunto agreed, so that it rested only to know what the master of the moonlight our consort would do herein. But when we demanded them if they would accompany us in that new determination, they alleged that their weak and leaky ship was not able to continue it; wherefore the same night we parted, leaving the moonlight to go directly for England, and the Admiral set his course for Trinidad, which course we kept two days.

The Return Voyage Home
On the 28 the wind changed, and it was set on foul weather every way: but this storm brought the wind West and Northwest, and blew so forcibly, that we were able to bear no sail, but our fore course half mast high, wherewith we ran upon the wind perforce, the due course for England, for that we were driven to change our first determination for Trinidad, and stood for the Islands of Azores, where we purposed to take in fresh water, and also there hoped to meet

with some English men of war about those Islands, at whose hands we might obtain some supply of our wants. . . .

The 2nd of October in the morning we saw S. Michael's Island on our Starboard quarter.

The 23rd at 10 of the clock afore noon, we saw Ushant in Britain.

On Saturday the 24 we came in safety, God be thanked, to an anchor at Plymouth.

Instructions for the Jamestown Colony

King James I

Virginia was founded during the reign of Elizabeth I, the "Virgin Queen" for whom Sir Walter Raleigh christened the colony. The first attempts at settlement were failures, culminating in the disastrous and still unsolved disappearance of the Roanoke settlers in 1590. Under James I, however, England's colonial endeavor gained new momentum. The king authorized a group of investors including noblemen and merchants, to establish a settlement in Virginia, which would fittingly be called Jamestown. On May 6, 1607, Captain Christopher Newport and his three ships the *Susan Constant,* the *Godspeed,* and the *Discovery* arrived in Virginia to build anew.

The 105 Jamestown colonists seemed to be armed not only with royal sponsorship but also with a keen awareness of the pitfalls that had foiled their predecessors. The following document, from 1606 issued ostensibly by the king but likely written by London backers who had stayed behind, was opened by Captain Newport upon arrival in Virginia. These instructions to the new colonists reflect the Virginia Company's intent to avoid the mistakes the Elizabethans had made.

The document dispenses practical advice about navigation, cultivation of land, and dealing with the native population, who were generally viewed with a combination of fear, contempt, and curiosity. The instructions also suggest that England's determination to establish a successful colony was as much driven by the imperial desire to compete with rivals Spain and France as by the ambitions of the

Excerpted from "Instructions for the Virginia Colony," by King James I, *Thomas Jefferson Papers Series 8*, edited by Thomas Jefferson (Richmond: Virginia Records Manuscripts, 1606–1737).

profit-minded Jamestown colonists themselves. In this respect, the document attests to the colonists' dual (if not yet competing) nationalistic and individualistic motives in making this second attempt to settle Virginia.

As you read, consider the following questions:
1. What do the instructions reveal about the particular hazards prior colonists encountered in Virginia? Which hazard seems to be of greatest concern for the current expedition—navigation, terrain, or the Native Americans?
2. What strategies for colonial order and cooperation do the instructions mandate? What assumptions about seventeenth-century hierarchy may be deduced?
3. According to the instructions, how ought the settlers represent themselves to the Native Americans? Why might it be important that the colonists not seem to be "but common men"?

As we doubt not but you will have especial care to observe the ordinances set down by the King's Majesty and delivered unto you under the Privy Seal; so for your better directions upon your first landing we have thought good to recommend unto your care these instructions and articles following.

When it shall please God to send you on the coast of Virginia, you shall do your best endeavour to find out a safe port in the entrance of some navigable river, making choice of such a one as runneth farthest into the land, and if you happen to discover divers portable rivers, and amongst them any one that hath two main branches, if the difference be not great, make choice of that which bendeth most toward the North-West for that way you shall soonest find the other sea.

Choosing the Right Location
When you have made choice of the river on which you mean to settle, be not hasty in landing your victuals and

munitions; but first let Captain Newport discover how far that river may be found navigable, that you make election of the strongest, most wholesome and fertile place; for if you make many removes, besides the loss of time, you shall greatly spoil your victuals and your cask, and with great pain transport it in small boats.

But if you choose your place so far up as a bark of fifty tuns will float, then you may lay all your provisions ashore with ease, and the better receive the trade of all the countries about you in the land; and such a place you may perchance find a hundred miles from the river's mouth, and the further up the better. For if you sit down near the entrance, except it be in some island that is strong by nature, an enemy that may approach you on even ground, may easily pull you out; and if he be driven to seek you a hundred miles [in] the land in boats, you shall from both sides of the river where it is narrowest, so beat them with your muskets as they shall never be able to prevail against you.

And to the end that you be not surprised as the French were in Florida by Melindus, and the Spaniard in the same place by the French, you shall do well to make this double provision. First, erect a little store at the mouth of the river that may lodge some ten men; with whom you shall leave a light boat, that when any fleet shall be in sight, they may come with speed to give you warning. Secondly, you must in no case suffer any of the native people of the country to inhabit between you and the sea coast; for you cannot carry yourselves so towards them, but they will grow discontented with your habitation, and be ready to guide and assist any nation that shall come to invade you; and if you neglect this, you neglect your safety.

To Each Colonist a Role

When you have discovered as far up the river as you mean to plant yourselves, and landed your victuals and munitions; to the end that every man may know his charge, you shall do well to divide your six score men into three parts; whereof one party of them you may appoint to fortify and build, of which your first work must be your storehouse for victuals; the other you may imploy in preparing your ground and sowing your corn and roots; the other ten of these forty you must leave as sentinel at the haven's mouth. The other forty you may employ for two months in discovery of the river above you, and on the country about you; which charge Captain Newport and Captain [Bartholomew] Gosnold may undertake of these forty discoverers. When they do espy any high lands or hills, Captain Gosnold may take twenty of the company to cross over the lands, and carrying a half dozen pickaxes to try if they can find any minerals. The other twenty may go on by river, and pitch up boughs upon the bank's side, by which the other boats shall follow them by the same turnings. You may also take with them a wherry [a light boat], such as is used here in the Thames; by which you may send back to the President for supply of munition or any other want, that you may not be driven to return for every small defect.

You must observe if you can, whether the river on which you plant doth spring out of mountains or out of lakes. If it be out of any lake, the passage to the other sea will be more easy, and [it] is like enough, that out of the same lake you shall find some spring which run[s] the contrary way towards the East India Sea; for the great and famous rivers of Volga, Tan[a]is and Dwina have three heads near joined; and yet the one falleth into the Caspian Sea, the other into the Euxine Sea, and the third into the Paelonian Sea.

Dealing with the Natives

In all your passages you must have great care not to offend the naturals [natives], if you can eschew it; and imploy some few of your company to trade with them for corn and all other . . . victuals if you have any; and this you must do before that they perceive you mean to plant among them; for not being sure how your own seed corn will prosper the first year, to avoid the danger of famine, use and endeavour to store yourselves of the country corn.

Your discoverers that pass over land with hired guides,

must look well to them that they slip not from them: and for more assurance, let them take a compass with them, and write down how far they go upon every point of the compass; for that country having no way nor path, if that your guides run from you in the great woods or desert, you shall hardly ever find a passage back.

And how weary soever your soldiers be, let them never trust the country people with the carriage of their weapons; for if they run from you with your shot [muskets], which they only fear, they will easily kill them all with their arrows. And whensoever any of yours shoots before them, be sure they may be chosen out of your best marksmen; for if they see your learners miss what they aim at, they will think the weapon not so terrible, and thereby will be bold to assault you.

Above all things, do not advertise the killing of any of your men, that the country people may know it; if they perceive that they are but common men, and that with the loss of many of theirs they diminish any part of yours, they will make many adventures upon you. If the country be populous, you shall do well also, not to let them see or know of your sick men, if you have any; which may also encourage them to many enterprises.

Establishing the Plantation

You must take especial care that you choose a seat for habitation that shall not be over burdened with woods near your town; for all the men you have, shall not be able to cleanse twenty acres a year; besides that it may serve for a covert for your enemies round about.

Neither must you plant in a low or moist place, because it will prove unhealthful. You shall judge of the good air by the people; for some part of that coast where the lands are low, have their people blear eyed, and with swollen bellies and legs; but if the naturals be strong and clean made, it is a true sign of a wholesome soil.

You must take order to draw up the pinnace that is left with you, under the fort: and take her sails and anchors ashore, all but a small kedge [a vessel pulled by ropes from shore] to ride by; least some ill-dispositioned persons slip away with her.

You must take care that your mariners that go for wages, do not mar your trade; for those that mind not to inhabit, for a little gain will debase the estimation of exchange, and hinder the trade for ever after; and therefore you shall not admit or suffer any person whatsoever, other than such as shall be appointed by the President and Counsel there, to buy any merchandises or other things whatsoever.

It were necessary that all your carpenters and other such like workmen about building do first build your storehouse and those other rooms of public and necessary use before any house be set up for any private person: and though the workman may belong to any private persons yet let them all work together first for the company and then for private men.

And seeing order is at the same price with confusion, it shall be advisably done to set your houses even and by a line, that your street may have a good breadth, and be carried square about your market place and every street's end opening into it; that from thence, with a few field pieces, you may command every street throughout; which market place you may also fortify if you think it needfull.

You shall do well to send a perfect relation by Captain Newport of all that is done, what height you are seated, how far into the land, what commodities you find, what soil, woods and their several kinds, and so of all other things else to advertise particularly; and to suffer no man to return but by passport from the President and Counsel, nor to write any letter of anything that may discourage others.

Lastly and chiefly the way to prosper and achieve good success is to make yourselves all of one mind for the good of your country and your own, and to serve and fear God the Giver of all Goodness, for every plantation which our Heavenly Father hath not planted shall be rooted out.

Thanksgiving at Plymouth Colony

Edward Winslow

The Virginia Company charter of 1606 had also authorized a New England settlement, but attempts to form a colony had failed, and James issued a new charter to the Plymouth Company in 1620. The pilgrims who made up the Plymouth Company sailed for the New World in that year. They landed north of Cape Cod where they established their colony.

The Indians of New England were integral to the survival of the pilgrims of Plymouth. The pilgrims' first winter was harsh, with little more than half of the colonists living to see spring. The colony itself might have died out were it not for the help of an Indian named Squanto from a nearby Patuxet village. Squanto, who had been to Europe and back courtesy of a Spanish abductor, spoke English and mediated between the pilgrims and other Native Americans. He assisted the colonists in planting corn and finding the best places to fish. In 1621 the pilgrims struck a treaty with Massasoit, chief of the Wampanoags the dominant tribe in the region), ensuring mutual peace and friendship.

The first Thanksgiving was a feast celebrating the success of the 1621 harvest, in part due to Indian aid. In a letter to an unnamed friend, pilgrim Edward Winslow wrote of the feast. Winslow, in the following selection, details the three-day feast, including its menu, Indian guests (including Massasoit), and its purpose, all of which subsequently served as a model for the modern Thanksgiving holiday. Winslow's letter was published the next year in *Mourt's Relation* (1622), a book written by Winslow with fellow Ply-

Excerpted from *Mourt's Relation*, by Edward Winslow (London: George Mourton, 1622).

mouth settler William Bradford and published by George
Morton (to whose name the title refers).

As you read, consider the following questions:
1. The pilgrims were basically a religious community, English Separatists who espoused Puritan beliefs What role
   does Winslow see God as having played in the colony's
   fortunes, including their harmonious relations with the
   Indians?
2. Winslow makes only passing references to the initial hardships the Plymouth colony suffered. Why do you imagine
   he prefers to send word back to London of the colony's
   promise? How might his readers back in England envision
   the Plymouth Colony after reading his account?
3. How does Winslow's description of the Native Americans
   differ from that of Ralph Lane? What adjectives, for example, do Winslow and Lane use to describe the Indians?

Loving, and old Friend,
   Although I received no letter from you by this ship, yet
forasmuch as I know you expect the performance of my
promise, which was, to write unto you truly and faithfully
of all things, I have therefore at this time sent unto you accordingly. Referring you for further satisfaction to our
more large relations.
   You shall understand, that in this little time, that a few
of us have been here, we have built seven dwelling-houses,
and four for the use of the plantation, and have made
preparation for divers others. We set the last spring some
twenty acres of Indian corn, and sowed some six acres of
barley and peas, and according to the manner of the Indians, we manured our ground with herrings or rather shads,
which we have in great abundance, and take with great
ease at our doors. Our corn did prove well, and God be
praised, we had a good increase of Indian corn, and our
barley indifferent good, but our peas not worth the gather-
ing, for we feared they were too late sown, they came up

very well, and blossomed, but the sun parched them in the blossom.

The Shared Harvest Celebration

Our harvest being gotten in, our governor sent four men on fowling, that so we might after have a special manner rejoice together after we had gathered the fruit of our labors; they four in one day killed as much fowl, as with a little help beside, served the company almost a week, at which time amongst other recreations, we exercised our arms, many of the Indians coming amongst us, and among the rest their greatest King Massasoit, with some ninety men, whom for three days we entertained and feasted, and they went out and killed five deer, which they brought to the plantation and bestowed on our governor, and upon the captain, and others. And although it be not always so plentiful as it was at this time with us, yet by the goodness of God, we are so far from want that we often wish you partakers of our plenty.

We have found the Indians very faithful in their covenant of peace with us; very loving and ready to pleasure us; we often go to them, and they come to us; some of us have been fifty miles by land in the country with them, the occasions and relations whereof you shall understand by our general and more full declaration of such things as are worth the noting, yea, it has pleased God so to possess the Indians with a fear of us, and love unto us, that not only the greatest king amongst them, called Massasoit, but also all the princes and peoples round about us, have either made suit unto us, or been glad of any occasion to make peace with us, so that seven of them at once have sent their messengers to us to that end. Yea, an Isle at sea, which we never saw, hath also, together with the former, yielded willingly to be under the protection, and subjects to our sovereign lord King James, so that there is now great peace amongst the Indians themselves, which was not formerly, neither would have been but for us; and we for our parts walk as peaceably and safely in the wood as in the highways in England.

We entertain them familiarly in our houses, and they as friendly bestowing their venison on us. They are a people without any religion or knowledge of God, yet very trusty, quick of apprehension, ripe-witted, just. The men and women go naked, only a skin about their middles.

A Land of Abundance

For the temper of the air, here it agrees well with that in England, and if there be any difference at all, this is somewhat hotter in summer, some think it to be colder in winter, but I cannot out of experience so say; the air is very clear and not foggy, as hath been reported. I never in my life remember a more seasonable year than we have here enjoyed; and if we have once but kind, horses, and sheep, I make no question but men might live as contented here as in any part of the world. For fish and fowl, we have great abundance; fresh cod in the summer is but coarse meat with us; our bay is full of lobsters all the summer and afforded variety of other fish; in September we can take a hogshead of eels in a night, with small labor, and can dig them out of their beds all the winter; we have mussels and othus at our doors: oysters we have none near, but we can have them brought by the Indians when we will; all the spring-time the earth sendeth forth naturally very good sallet herbs: here are grapes, white and red, and very sweet and strong also. Strawberries, gooseberries, raspas, etc. Plums of three sorts, with black and red, being almost as good as a damson: abundance of roses, white, red, and damask; single, but very sweet indeed. The country wanteth only industrious men to employ, for it would grieve your hearts (if as I) you had seen so many miles together by goodly rivers uninhabited, and withal, to consider those parts of the world wherein you live to be even greatly burdened with abundance of people. These things I thought good to let you understand, being the truth of things as near as I could experimentally take knowledge of, and that you might on our behalf give God thanks who hath dealt so favorably with us.

Our supply of men from you came the ninth of November 1621, putting in at Cape Cod, some eight or ten leagues from us. The Indians that dwell thereabout were they who were owners of the corn which we found in caves, for which we have given them full content, and are in great league with them. They sent us word that there was a ship near unto them, but thought it to be a Frenchman, and indeed for ourselves, we expected not a friend so soon. But when we perceived that she made for our bay, the governor commanded a great piece to be shot off, to call home such as were abroad at work; whereupon every man, yea, boy that could handle a gun, were ready, with full resolution that if she were an enemy, we would stand in our just defense, not fearing them, but God provided better for us than we supposed; these came all in health, not any being sick by the way (otherwise than sea sickness) and so continue at this time, by the blessing of God; the good-wife Ford was delivered of a son the first night she landed, and both of them are very well.

Promise for the Future of Plymouth

When it pleaseth God, we are settled and fitted for the fishing business, and other trading; I doubt not but by the blessing of God the gain will give content to all; in the mean time, that we have gotten we have sent by this ship, and though it be not much, yet it will witness for us that we have not been idle, considering the smallness of our number all this summer. We hope the merchants will accept of it, and be encouraged to furnish us with things needful for further employment, which will also encourage us to put forth ourselves to the uttermost.

Now because I expect your coming unto us with other of our friends, whose company we much desire, I thought good to advertise you of a few things needful; be careful to have a very good bread-room to put your biscuits in, let your cask for beer and water be iron-bound for the first tire if not more; let not your meat be dry-salted, none can better do it than the sailors; let your meal be so hard trod in your cask that you shall need an adz or hatchet to work it out with: trust not too much on us for corn at this time, for by reason of this last company that came, depending wholly upon us, we shall have little enough till harvest; be careful to come by some of your meal to spend by the way, it will much refresh you. Build your cabins as open as you can, and bring good store of clothes and bedding with you; bring every man a musket or fowling-piece, let your piece be long in the barrel, and fear not the weight of it, for most of our shooting is from stands; bring juice of lemons, and take it fasting; it is of good use; for hot waters, aniseed water is the best, but use it sparingly; if you bring any thing for comfort in the country, butter or sallet oil, or both is very good; our Indian corn, even the coarsest, maketh pleasant meat as rice, therefore spare that unless to spend by the way; bring paper and linseed oil for your windows, with cotton yarn for your lamps; let your shot be most for big fowls, and bring store of powder and shot: I forbear further to write for the present, hoping to see you by the next return, so I take my leave, commending you to the Lord for a safe conduct unto us. Resting in Him,

Your loving friend,

E.W. [Edward Winslow]

Plymouth in New England this 11th of December, 1621.

2

COLONIAL ACCOUNTS OF NATIVE AMERICANS

CHAPTER PREFACE

The first European colonists regarded the Native Americans with ambivalent, often contradictory attitudes. Because their primary aim was to utilize the land's resources, the settlers mainly saw the Indians as potential obstacles to be conquered either through persuasion or coercion. Cooperation was usually a means rather than an end, as the colonists depended on the Native Americans for help in cultivating crops, negotiating the unfamiliar terrain, and locating the best sites and methods for hunting, fishing, and trapping. But despite Chief Powhatan's entreaty, "What will it avail you to take that by force [that which] you may quickly have by love, or destroy them that provide you food?" the English frequently thought nothing of taking their Indian neighbors hostage or even killing them for real and imagined offenses, however trivial. The destruction wrought upon the Native Americans by the colonists was not always intentional; the Europeans also brought with them such diseases as plague and smallpox, against which the Indians had no immunity. However, few colonists seemed especially regretful about the often devastating effects of disease on the indigenous people. Pilgrim William Bradford observed that such epidemics were divinely ordained, working to the benefit of the settlers, remarking that "it pleased God to visit these Indians with a great sickness, and such a mortality that of a 1000. Above 900 and a half of them died, and many of them did rot above ground for want of burial."

Indeed, as Bradford's comment demonstrates, exploitation and even extermination of the Indians were often justified by religious prejudice. Even more benevolent Europeans tended to view Native Americans not just with curiosity but as curiosities themselves, either as strange and exotic animals or as childlike, simpleminded people in need of Christian civilization.

The Indians resisted, especially as the settlers continued to encroach on their lands, resources, and self-government. Although the Plymouth settlers had established friendly relations with the Pawtuxet and Wampanoag tribes, the peace treaty struck with Massasoit was strained by the colonists' paranoia as news reached them of violence in Virginia, such as the Jamestown Massacre of 1622. The Pequot War broke out in 1636, a bloody two-year conflict that resulted in the Puritans' effective extermination of the southern Connecticut tribe. King Philip's War (1675–1676), during which colonist Mary Rowlandson was abducted and held captive, was led by Metacomet, the younger son of Massasoit. The last major English-Indian conflict in New England, the war exacted a grievous toll on both sides, with around six hundred English and three thousand Native Americans slain, many of them women and children. Ultimately, the native peoples across the continent would be outmanned, outgunned, and subjugated by the Anglo-Europeans, but not without a significant cost to both the conquerors and especially the conquered.

The Natives Will Both Fear and Love Us

Thomas Hariot

Thomas Hariot, one of the original colonists of Roanoke, was among the most accomplished early Englishmen to explore the New World. Mathematician, scientist, historian, astronomer, and inventor, Hariot was part of the Elizabethan intellectual circle that included Christopher Marlowe, George Chapman, and Sir Walter Raleigh. He was only twenty-five when at Raleigh's behest, he sailed off for Virginia with Grenville, Ralph Lane, and over one hundred others, including the two Indians, Wanchese and Manteo, who had previously been brought to England from the New World.

Hariot's *Brief and True Report,* published in 1588, chronicles his activities during his year on Roanoke Island (he had returned with the other colonists with Drake in 1586). He meticulously describes the land's natural resources, assessing them in light of the colonists' needs, but of equal interest to him were the natives. Although the Roanoke colonists eventually (mainly by their own fault) fell out with the Indians, Hariot's report demonstrates his scientific and even ethnological interest in them. His account exhibits as well, perhaps unsurprisingly, a typical colonialist overconfidence in European superiority and an especial fascination with "heathen superstitions," as colonists commonly viewed Native American religious beliefs. Hariot returned to England with the other colonists when Roanoke was abandoned in 1586.

Excerpted from *A Brief and True Report of the New Found Land of Virginia Directed to the Investors, Farmers, and Well-Wishers of the Project of Colonizing and Planting There,* by Thomas Hariot (London, 1588).

As you read, consider the following questions:

1. Consider Hariot's statement that he believes the Indians "will have cause both to fear and to love us." On what assumptions about the Native Americans does he base this belief?

2. Hariot, Raleigh, and their intellectual circle were considered by some conservative Englishmen to be "dangerous freethinkers" who disdained biblical orthodoxy. With this in mind, examine Hariot's attitude about the Indians' religion, which is sometimes condescending, other times almost respectful. What common grounds does he seem to find between the Indians' religion and Christian beliefs?

3. How does Hariot characterize the Indians' attitudes toward the English? Are they wary, gullible, fearful, cooperative? What overall sense does the narrative project about the complex nature of Indian-English interactions?

It remains to speak a word or two about the native inhabitants, their nature and manners, leaving detailed discourse about them until a later, more convenient time. Now it is only necessary to reassure you that they are not to be feared. I do not think they will trouble our living there or obstruct our farming. I rather believe that they will have cause both to fear and to love us.

The clothing of the natives consists of loose deerskin mantles and aprons of the same fur which they wear around their waists; they wear nothing else. In stature they differ one from another, much as we do in England. They have no edged tools or weapons of iron or steel to attack us with, nor do they know how to make them. The only weapons they possess are bows made of witch hazel, arrows made of reeds, and flat-edged wooden truncheons, which are about a yard long. For defense they wear armor made of sticks whickered together with thread, and they carry shields made of bark.

Their towns are small and few, especially near the seacoast, where a village may contain but ten or twelve houses—

some perhaps as many as twenty. The largest town we saw had thirty houses. In many cases the villages are walled with stakes covered with the bark of trees or with poles set close together.

The houses are built of small poles attached at the top to make them round in shape, much like the arbors in our English gardens. The poles are covered from top to bottom either with bark or with mats woven of long rushes. The dwellings are usually twice as long as they are wide; sometimes they are only twelve or sixteen yards long, but we have seen them as much as twenty-four yards in length.

Native Government and Warriors

In one part of the country a Weroans, or chief, may govern a single town, but in other parts the number of towns under one chief may vary to two, three, six, and even to eight or more. The greatest Weroans we met governed eighteen towns, and he could muster seven or eight hundred warriors. The language of each chief's territory differs from that of the others, and the farther apart they are, the greater the differences.

Their manner of making war against each other is by a surprise attack, either in the dawn of day or by moonlight, by ambush, or by some such subtle trick. Set battles are very rare. When they do take place, it is always in the forests, where the natives may defend themselves by leaping behind a tree after they have shot their arrows.

If we should ever fight the inhabitants, the results can easily be imagined. We have great advantages over them, for we have disciplined soldiers, strange weapons, devices of all sorts, and especially we have large and small ordnance. So far we found their best defense against us was to turn on their heels and run away.

The Nature of Their Gods

Compared with us, the natives are poor. They lack skill and judgment in using the materials we have and esteem trifles above things of greater value. But if we consider that they lack our means, they are certainly very ingenious. Although they do not possess any of our tools, or crafts, or sciences, or art, yet in their own way they show excellent sense. In time they will find that our kinds of knowledge and crafts accomplish everything with more speed and perfection than do theirs. Therefore, when they realize this, they will most probably desire our friendship and love, and, respecting our achievements, they will try to please and obey us. Whereby, if we govern them well, they will in a short time become civilized and embrace the true religion.

They have already a religion of their own, which is far from the truth, yet for that reason there is hope that it may sooner and more easily be reformed.

They believe in many gods, which they call Mantoac. These gods are of different kinds and degrees. Their chief god has existed from all eternity. They affirm that when he created the world, he first made the other principal gods, in order to use them in the creation and government to follow. Then he made the sun, the moon, and the stars. The petty gods act as instruments of the more important ones. The natives say that the waters of the world were made first and that out of these all creatures, both visible and invisible, were formed.

As to the creation of mankind, they think that the woman came first. She conceived and brought forth children fathered by one of the gods, and in this way the natives had their beginning. But how many ages or years have passed since then, they do not know, for they have no writing or any means of keeping records of past time, only the tradition, passed on from father to son.

They believe that all the gods have human shapes; therefore they represent them by images in the form of men and call the images Kewasowok. A single god is called Kewas. These images are set up in temples which they call Machicomuck. Here the natives worship, pray, sing, and make frequent offerings to the gods. In some of these temples we saw only one Kewas, but others had two or three. Most of the natives think that the images themselves are the gods.

The Soul and Immortality

The natives believe also in the immortality of the soul. They say that after this life the soul departs from the body, and, according to its works in life, it is either carried to heaven, where the gods live, or else to a great pit or hole. In heaven it enjoys perpetual bliss and happiness, but in the pit, which is situated at the farthest part of their world toward the sunset, it burns continually; this place they call Popogusso.

In confirmation of this belief, they told me stories about two persons who had lately died and revived again. One occasion was but a few years before we came to Virginia and concerned a wicked man who died and was buried. The day after the burial the natives saw that the earth of his grave had begun to move, and took him up again. The man made a declaration, saying that his soul had been about to enter into Popogusso, when one of the gods had saved him and given him leave to return to earth to teach his friends what they should do to avoid that terrible place of torment.

The other event happened during the year we were in Virginia in a town only about threescore miles away. Again a dead man had been buried and had returned to the earth. He related that his soul had traveled far along a wide road, on both sides of which grew the most delicate and pleasant trees, bearing rare and excellent fruits of such fine qualities that he could scarcely describe them. At length he came to some beautiful houses, where he met his dead father. The father instructed him to go back to earth and to tell his friends that he was enjoying the pleasures of heaven, and after he had done so to return.

Religion and Society

Whether or not the Weroans and priests use subtle devices with the common people, the belief in heaven and the fiery pit makes the simple folk give strict obedience to their governors and behave with great care, so that they may avoid torment after death and enjoy bliss. Evil-doers have to pay for their crimes in this world, nevertheless. Thievery, whoremongering, and other wicked acts are punished with fines, beatings, or even with death, according to the seriousness of the offense.

This sums up their religion. I learnt of it from some of their priests with whom I became friendly. They are not fully convinced of its truth, for in conversing with us they began to doubt their own traditions and stories. They expressed great admiration for our religion, and many showed an earnest desire to learn more than we, with our small knowledge of their language, were able to tell them about it.

They marveled at all that we had, such as mathematical instruments, mariner's compasses, the loadstone, which attracted iron, a perspective glass, in which they saw many strange sights, burning glasses, fireworks, guns, books, and spring clocks that seemed to go by themselves. All these things were beyond their comprehension, just as reading and writing were utterly strange to them. They could not understand how they were constructed and how they worked and thought all these things must have been made by the gods or that the gods must have presented them and taught us how to make them. Therefore they began to admire us and thought it wise to learn the meaning of the true God and the true religion. Seeing our abilities and possessions, they believed more readily in our words.

Their Response to the Bible

Many times and in every town I came to I described the contents of the Bible as often as I could. I told the natives that there was set forth the only true GOD and His mighty works, with the true doctrine of salvation through Christ. I related the miracles and the chief points of religion to them, as many as I thought fit and could recount at the time. And although I told them that the book itself had no great virtue, but only the doctrine it contained, still they wished to touch, embrace, and kiss it, and to hold it to their breasts and heads and stroke their whole bodies with it. Thus did they show their hungry desire for its knowledge.

Wingina, the chief with whom we lived, and many of his people joined us often at our prayers. He called upon us many times, both in his village and in other villages where he accompanied us, to pray and to sing Psalms, hoping thereby to benefit from the effects we also expected from those means.

On two different occasions this Weroans was so seriously ill that he seemed likely to die. As he lay languishing, he doubted that his own priests could help him; therefore he sent for us and asked us to pray to our God that he might either live or dwell in bliss with Him after death. And not only he but also many other natives asked us to pray for them.

Another time their corn began to wither because of an unusual drought. They feared that this had come to pass because they had displeased us in some way. A few of them came to us asking that we should pray to our English God that he should preserve their corn, and they promised that when it was ripe they would share the harvest with us. Whenever they suffered from some sickness, loss, accident, or other misfortune, they believed that this came to pass because they had offended or displeased us.

A Fortunate Coincidence

Before I come to the end of my narrative I want to mention one other rare and strange occurrence which moved the inhabitants of the whole country to a wonderful admiration for us. When trickery was practiced against us in any town, we were careful to leave it unpunished, because we wanted to win the friendship of the natives through gentleness. But strangely it happened that within a few days of our departure the people began to die very fast. In some towns twenty people died, in some forty, in some sixty, and in one six score; this was a large portion of the inhabitants. And the strange thing was that this occurred only in towns where we had been and where they had done some mischief against us, and it happened always after we had left. The disease with which they were stricken was so strange a one that they did not know anything about it or how to cure it. Even their elders could not remember the like ever having happened before. After this disease had struck in four or five places, some of our native friends, especially Chief Wingina, were persuaded that it was we who brought it about, helped by our God. They thought that through Him we were able to slay anyone at any place and without the use of weapons.

From that time on, whenever they heard that any of their enemies had abused us on our journeys and that we had not punished them, they begged us to let our God bring about the death of these enemies. This they alleged would be to our credit and profit, as well as to theirs, and they hoped we would grant their request because of the friendship we professed for them. We explained that such entreaties were ungodly and that our God would not be ruled by such prayers and requests from men; rather, all things are done according to His pleasure and as He ordains. We said that we ought to pray to Him, on the contrary, to show ourselves His true servants and ask that these enemies might know His truth and serve Him in righteousness, so that they could live together with us. And we told them that everything would be done in accordance with the divine will and pleasure of God, as He ordained to be best in His wisdom.

Their Awe and Fear About the English

It happened that shortly after this the disease struck their enemies just as they had desired. They thought we had brought it about, disguising our intentions from them. They thanked us profoundly for fulfilling their wish even though we had not promised to do so.

Because of this marvelous accident all the natives throughout the country began to have a wonderful opinion of us, and they were not sure whether to consider us gods or men. Their wonderment increased when they saw that not one of our number became ill during their sickness, nor did any of us die. They also noted that we had no women with us, nor did we care for any of theirs. Some of them were of the opinion that we were not born of woman and were therefore not mortal but were men of a past generation who had risen again to immortality.

They prophesied that more of our generation would yet come to this country to kill them and to take away their homes. They imagined that these men who were to arrive they shot invisible bullets into the victims who died in their villages, after us were already in the air, invisible and without bodies, and that inflicting this punishment at our instigation because they loved us.

And as their medicine men could not cure the strange disease, they tried to excuse their ignorance by shamefully encouraging the simple people to believe that the death was caused by invisible bullets. To prove it they sucked strings of blood out of the sick bodies and said these were the strings to which the bullets were attached.

"Invisible Bullets"

Yet some of the natives did not believe in the invisible bullets. They thought that we shot our enemies from a distance, killing anyone who offended us, no matter how far away he was. Still others said it was the work of God for our sakes, and we ourselves had reason to agree with them, no matter what other causes there might be. Astrologers believed that the reason of these strange happenings might be the eclipse of the sun which we saw during our outward voyage, or it might be caused by a comet which appeared a few days before the sickness began. But I do not myself think that these outward causes brought about these special accidents. There must have been other reasons, on which I will not speculate at present.

Thus, I have given the opinions of the native inhabitants in detail to show you that there is good hope that they may be brought to embrace the truth through discreet handling and wise government and consequently will come to honor, obey, fear, and love us. Although towards the end of the year some of our men were too harsh with them and killed a few of their number for offenses which might easily have been forgiven, still the natives thought the punishment just and did not change their friendly attitude toward us. I do not believe that they are likely to change their general good opinion of us, and if we are careful at all, they need not be feared. Nevertheless, we must hope for the best and try to do our best, taking care to remove the causes for any discontent among them.

There Is No Need for Conflict Between Our Peoples

Powhatan

Powhatan is perhaps best known as the father of Pocahontas, but by all accounts he seems to have been a powerful and judicious chief of the federation of tribes usually referred to by his name. The following selection, taken from a speech that Powhatan gave to Captain John Smith in 1609, reveals much about the chief's attitude toward the English colonists. Both in his previous encounters with Captain Christopher Newport on the earlier expedition and later, in his dealings with the Jamestown settlers, Powhatan seems to have regarded the English with a mixture of wariness and pragmatism. While recognizing the colonists' reliance on the Native Americans for corn and other provisions, the chief also perceived the Europeans' essential antipathy to people and their way of life, although Powhatan did give his blessings to Pocahontas's 1614 marriage to John Rolfe (this even after her abduction earlier that same year by the English). Powhatan outlived his daughter by a year, succumbing in 1618. He was succeeded by his brother Opechancanough, who adopted a pointedly more antagonistic stance toward the colonists.

As you read, consider the following questions:
1. What is Powhatan's tone toward the colonists in the selection? Humble? Proud? Emotional? Rational?
2. Similarly, what do Powhatan's words reveal about his perception of English attitudes toward the Indians? What

Excerpted from Powhatan's speech to Captain John Smith, 1609.

prejudices on the part of the colonists may he be trying to change?

3. Compare Powhatan's speech with any of the other characterizations of Native Americans in this collection. How accurate do some of those characterizations seem to you in light of your reading Powhatan's speech?

"I . . . exhort you to peaceable councils"

I am now grown old, and must soon die; and the succession must descend, in order, to my brothers, Opitchapan, Opekankanough, and Catataugh, and then to my two sisters, and their two daughters. I wish their experience was equal to mine; and that your love to us might not be less than ours to you. Why should you take by force that from us which you can have by love? Why should you destroy us, who have provided you with food? What can you get by war? We can hide our provisions, and fly into the woods; and then you must consequently famish by wronging your friends. What is the cause of your jealousy? You see us unarmed, and willing to supply your wants, if you will come in a friendly manner, and not with swords and guns, as to invade on an enemy. I am not so simple, as not to know it is better to eat good meat, lie well, and sleep quietly with my women and children, to laugh and be merry with the English; and, being their friend, to have copper, hatchets, and whatever else I want, than to fly from all, to lie cold in the woods, feed upon acorns, roots, and such trash, and to be so hunted, that I cannot rest, eat, or sleep. In such circumstances, my men must watch, and if a twig should but break, all would cry out, "Here comes Capt. Smith"; and so, in this miserable manner, to end my miserable life; and, Capt. Smith, this might be soon your fate too, through your rashness and unadvisedness. I, therefore, exhort [urge] you to peaceable councils; and, above all, I insist that the guns and swords, the cause of all our jealousy and uneasiness, be removed and sent away.

The Admirable Qualities of an Uncivilized People

Thomas Morton

The first colonists often exhibited a surprising diversity of opinions about the Native Americans they encountered. Some of the early English descriptions are clearly more fanciful than factual, painting a people with bizarre physical characteristics barely recognizable as human. No doubt these accounts were composed with a credulous, popular audience in mind as well as to impress royal patrons with the explorers' own derring-do. Yet other accounts seem to emphasize the humanity of the Indians—however "savage"—that bound them to their European brethren. Certainly the settlers recognized that it was in their own self-interest to cultivate civil, even friendly, relations with the Native Americans. Aside from avoiding the physical perils resulting from direct hostility, cooperation with the Indians could be a source of valuable assistance with farming, hunting, and negotiating the often dangerously unfamiliar terrain.

The following selection, composed in 1637 by colonist and adventurer Thomas Morton (ca. 1575–1647) presents a relatively enlightened and genial view of Indians he encountered in New England. Morton's description of primitive dwellings and customs is tempered by a respect for the practicality and even the civility of Native American society. While he indulges in several popular stereotypes about their susceptibility to drunkenness and "heathen" superstitions, he also claims that the Indians' benevolence, respect for elders, and imperviousness to frivolous commodities compare favorably to the values of many Europeans.

Excerpted from *A New English Canaan,* by Thomas Morton (Amsterdam, 1637).

As you read, consider the following questions:

1. What are the stereotypes that Morton seems to anticipate his readers already may have about the Indians? In what ways does his account both challenge and reinforce these stereotypes?
2. Consider the qualities that Morton most seems to admire about the Indians. What might they reveal about his own values and beliefs, not just about the Native Americans but also about his own society?
3. Compare Morton's attitudes toward the Indians to Hariot's. What are their shared assumptions about the Native Americans? How do their particular areas of interest shape differences in their accounts?

Of Their Houses and Habitations

The Natives of New England are accustomed to build them houses much like the wild Irish; they gather poles in the woods and put the great end of them in the ground, placing them in form of a circle or circumference, and, bending the tops of them in form of an arch, they bind them together with the bark of walnut trees, which is wondrous tough, so that they make the same round on the top for the smoke of their fire to ascend and pass through; . . . The fire is always made in the midst of the house, with wind falls commonly: yet some times they fell a tree that groweth near the house, and, by drawing in the end thereof, maintain the fire on both sides, burning the tree by degrees shorter and shorter, until it be all consumed; for it burneth night and day. Their lodging is made in three places of the house about the fire; they Lie upon planks, commonly about a foot or 18 inches above the ground, raised upon rails that are borne up upon forks; they lay mats under them, and coats of deer's skins, otters, beavers, raccoons, and of bears hides, all which they have dressed and converted into good leather, with the hair on, for their coverings: and in this manner they lie as warm as they desire. . . . For they are willing that any shall eat with them. Nay, if any one that shall come into their houses and there fall asleep, when they see him disposed to lie down, they will spread a matt for him of their own accord, and lay a roll of skins for a bolster, and let him lie. If he sleep until their meat be dished up, they will set a wooden bowl of meat by him that slept, and wake him saying, Cattup keene Meckin: That is, If you be hungry, there is meat for you, where if you will eat you may. Such is their humanity.

Likewise, when they are minded to remove, they carry away the mats with them; other materials the place adjoining will yield. They use not to winter and summer in one place, for that would be a reason to make fuel scarce; but, after the manner of the gentry of civilized natives, remove for their pleasures; some times to their hunting places, where they remain keeping good hospitality for that season; and sometimes to their fishing places, where they abide for that season likewise; and at the spring, when fish comes in plentifully, they have meetings from several places, where they exercise themselves in gaming and playing of juggling tricks and all manner of revels, which they are delighted in; [so] that it is admirable to behold what pastime they use of several kinds; every one striving to surpass each other. After this manner they spend their time. . . .

Of Their Reverence and Respect to Age

It is a thing to be admired, and indeed made a president, that a nation yet uncivilized should more respect age than some nations civilized, since there are so many precepts both of divine and humane writers extant to instruct more civil nations: in that particular, wherein they excel, the younger are always obedient unto the elder people, and at their commands in every respect without grumbling; in all counsels, (as therein they are circumspect to do their actions by advise and counsel, and not rashly or inconsiderately) the younger men's opinion shall be heard, but the old men's opinion and counsel embraced and followed: besides, as the elder feed and provide for the younger in infancy, do the younger, after being grown to years of manhood, provide for those that be aged; . . .

The consideration of these things, me thinks, should reduce some of our irregular young people of civilized nations, when this story shall come to their knowledge, to better manners, and make them ashamed of their former error in this kind, and to become hereafter more dutiful; which I, as a friend, (by observation having found,) have herein recorded for that purpose. . . .

Of Their Traffic and Trade One with Another

Although these people have not the use of navigation, whereby they may traffic as other nations, that are civilized, use to do, yet do they barter for such commodities as they have, and have a kind of beads instead of money, to buy withal such things as they want, which they call Wampumpeak [wampum]: and it is of two sorts, the one is white, the other is of a violet color. These are made of the shells of fish. The white with them is as silver with us; the other as our gold: and for these beads they buy and sell, not only amongst themselves, but even with us.

We have used to sell them any of our commodities for this Wampumpeak, because we know we can have beaver again of them for it: and these beads are currant [i.e., currency] in all the parts of New England, from one end of the coast to the other. . . .

Of Their Admirable Perfection in the Use of the Senses

This is a thing not only observed by me and diverse of the savages of New England, but, also, by the French men in Nova Francia [French region of North America; "New France"], and therefore I am the more encouraged to publish in this treatise my observation of them in the use of their senses: which is a thing that I should not easily have been induced to believe, if I myself had not been an eye witness of what I shall relate.

I have observed that the savages have the sense of seeing so far beyond any of our nation, that one would almost believe they had intelligence of the Devil sometimes, when they have told us of a ship at sea, which they have seen sooner by one hour, yea, two hours sail, then any English man that stood by of purpose to look out, their sight is so excellent. . . .

Of Their Petty Conjuring Tricks

If we do not judge amiss of these savages in accounting them witches, yet out of all question we may be bold to conclude them to be but weak witches, such of them as we call by the names of Powahs: some correspondency they have with the Devil out of all doubt, as by some of their actions, in which they glory, is manifested. Papasiquineo, that Sachem or Sagamore, is a Powah of great estimation amongst all kind of savages there: he is at their revels (which is the time when a great company of savages meet from several parts of the country, in amity with their neighbors) hath advanced his honor in his feats or juggling tricks (as I may right term them) to the admiration of the spectators, whom he endeavored to persuade that he would go under water to the further side of a river, too broad for any man to undertake with a breath, which thing he performed by swimming over, and deluding the company with casting a mist before their eyes that see him enter in and come out, but no part of the way he has been seen: likewise by our English, in the heat of all summer to make ice appear in a bowl of fair water; first, having the water set before him, he hath begun his incantation according to their usual custom, and before the same has been ended a thick cloud has darkened the air and, on a sudden, a thunder clap hath been heard that has amazed the natives; in an instant he hath showed a firm piece of ice to float in the midst of the bowl in the presence of the vulgar people, which doubtless was done by the agility of Satan, his consort.

And by means of these sleights, and such like trivial things as these, they gain such estimation amongst the rest of the savages that it is thought a very impious matter for any man to derogate from the words of these Powahs. In so much as he that should slight them, is thought to commit a crime no less heinous amongst them as sacrilege is with us. . . .

Of a Great Mortality That Happened Amongst the Natives

It fortuned some few years before the English came to inhabit at new Plymouth, in New England, that upon some distaste given in the Massachusetts bay by the Frenchmen, then trading there with the natives for beaver, they set upon the men at such advantage that they killed many of them, burned their ship, then riding at anchor by an island there, now called Peddocks Island, . . . they did keep them so long as they lived, only to sport themselves at them, and made these five Frenchmen fetch them wood and water, which is the general work that they require of a servant. One of these five men, out living the rest, had learned so much of their language as to rebuke them for their bloody deed, saying that God would be angry with them for it, and that he would in his displeasure destroy them; but the savages . . . replied and say that they were so many that God could not kill them.

But contrary-wise, in short time after the hand of God fell heavily upon them, with such a mortal stroke that they died on heaps as they lay in their houses; and the living, that were able to shift for themselves, would run away and let them die, and let their carcasses lie above the ground without burial. For in a place where many inhabited, there hath been but one left alive to tell what became of the rest; the living being (as it seems) not able to bury the dead, they were left for crows, kites and vermin to pray upon. And the bones and skulls upon the several places of their habitations made such a spectacle after my coming into those parts, that, as I traveled in that forrest near the Massachusetts, it seemed to me a new found Golgotha [a burial land, in reference to Mt. Calvary where Christ was crucified]. . . .

And this mortality was not ended when the Brownists [English religious dissidents] of new Plymouth were settled at Patuxet in New England: and by all likelihood the sickness that these Indians died of was the plague, as by conference with them since my arrival and habitation in those parts, I have learned. And by this means there is as yet but a small number of savages in New England, to that which hath been in former time, and the place is made so much the more fit for the English nation to inhabit in, and erect in it temples to the glory of God.

Of Their Religion

It has been a common received opinion from [Roman orator] Cicero, that there is no people so barbarous but have some worship or other. In this particular, I am not of opinion therein with Tully [Cicero]; and, surely, if he had been amongst those people so long as I have been, and conversed so much with them touching this matter of religion, he would have changed his opinion. Neither should we have found this error, amongst the rest, by the help of that wooden prospect. . . .

Of Their Acknowledgement of the Creation and the Immortality of the Soul

Although these savages are found to be without religion, law, and king (as Sir William Alexander [one of the Scottish founders of Novia Scotia] hath well observed,) yet are they not altogether without the knowledge of God (historically); for they have it amongst them by tradition that God made one man and one woman, and bade them live together and get children, kill deer, beasts, birds, fish and fowl, and what they would at their pleasure; and that their posterity was full of evil, and made God so angry that he let in the sea upon them, and drowned the greatest part of them, that were naughty men, (the Lord destroyed so) and they went to Sanaconquam, who feeds upon them (pointing to the center of the earth, where they imagine is the habitation of the Devil) the other, (which were not destroyed,) increased the world, and when they died (because they were good) went to the house of Kytan [the word Morton records for the supreme good Spirit or God], pointing to the setting of the sun; where they eat all manner of dainties, and never take pains (as now) to provide it.

Kytan makes provision (they say) and saves them that labor; and there they shall live with him forever, void of care.

And they are persuaded that Kytan is he that makes corn grow, trees grow, and all manner of fruits. . . .

I asked him [an Indian who had lived in Morton's house] who was a good man; his answer was, he that would not lie, nor steal.

These, with them, are all the capital crimes that can be imagined; all other are nothing in respect of those; and he that is free from these must live with Kytan for ever, in all manner of pleasure. . . .

Of Their Custom in Burning the Country and the Reason Thereof

The savages are accustomed to set fire of the country in all places where they come, and to burn it twice a year, viz.: at the spring, and the fall of the leaf. The reason that moves them to do so, is because it would other wise be so over-grown with underweeds that it would be all a coppice wood, and the people would not be able in any wise to pass through the country out of a beaten path. . . .

The burning of the grass destroys the underwoods, and so scorches the elder trees that it shrinks them, and hinders their growth very much: so that he that will look to find large trees and good timber, must [look] . . . to find them on the upland ground. . . .

And least their firing of the country in this manner should be an occasion of damnifying us, and endangering our habitations, we ourselves have used carefully about the same times to observe the winds, and fire the grounds about our own habitations; to prevent the damage that might happen by any neglect thereof, if the fire should come near those houses in our absence.

For, when the fire is once kindled, it dilates and spreads itself as well against, as with the wind; burning continually night and day, until a shower of rain falls to quench it.

And this custom of firing the country is the means to make it passable; and by that means the trees grow here and there as in our parks: and makes the country very beautiful and commodious.

Of Their Inclination to Drunkenness

Although drunkenness be justly termed a vice which the savages are ignorant of, yet the benefit is very great that comes to the planters by the sale of strong liquor to the savages, who are much taken with the delight of it; for they will pawn their wits, to purchase the acquaintance of it. Yet in all the commerce that I had with them, I never proffered them any such thing; nay, I would hardly let any of them have a dram, unless he were a Sachem, or a Winnaytue, that is a rich man . . . . But they say if I come to the northern parts of the country I shall have no trade, if I will not supply them with lusty liquors: it is the life of the trade in all those parts: for it so happened that thus a savage desperately killed himself; when he was drunk, a gun being charged and the cock up, he sets the mouth to his breast, and, putting back the trigger with his foot, shot himself dead.

That the Savages Live a Contented Life

A gentleman and a traveler, that had been in the parts of New England for a time, when he returned again, in his discourse of the country, wondered, (as he said,) that the natives of the land lived so poorly in so rich a country, like to our beggars in England. Surely that gentleman had not time or leisure while he was there truly to inform himself of the state of that country, and the happy life the savages would lead were they once brought to Christianity.

I must confess they want the use and benefit of navigation, (which is the very sinews of a flourishing Commonwealth,) yet are they supplied with all manner of needful things for the maintenance of life and livelihood. Food and raiment [clothing] are the chief of all that we make true use of; and of these they find no want, but have, and may have, them in a most plentiful manner.

If our beggars of England should, with so much ease as they, furnish themselves with food at all seasons, there would not be so many starved in the streets, neither would so many gaols [jails] be stuffed, or gallowses furnished with poor wretches, as I have seen them.

But they of this sort of our own nation, that are fit to go to this Canaan, are not able to transport themselves; and most of them unwilling to go from the good ale tap, which is the very loadstone of the land by which our English beggars steer their course; it is the north pole to which the flowre-de-luce [fleur de lis] of their compass points. The more is the pity that the commonalty of our land are of such leaden capacities as to neglect so brave a country, that doth so plentifully feed many lusty and brave, able men, women and children, that have not the means that a civilized nation hath to purchase food and raiment; which that country with a little industry will yield a man in a very comfortable measure, without overmuch carking [trouble].

I cannot deny but a civilized nation hath the preeminence of an uncivilized, by means of those instruments that are found to be common amongst civil people, and the uncivil want the use of, to make themselves masters of those ornaments that make such a glorious show. . . .

Now since it is but food and raiment that men that live needeth (though not all alike,) why should not the natives of New England be said to live richly, having no want of either? Clothes are the badge of sin; and the more variety of fashions is but the greater abuse of the creature: the beasts of the forest there do serve to furnish them at any time when they please: fish and flesh they have in great abundance, which they both roast and boil. . . .

I must needs commend them in this particular, that, though they buy many commodities of our nation, yet they keep but few, and those of special use.

They love not to be cumbered with many utensils, and although every proprietor knows his own, yet all things (so long as they will last), are used in common amongst them: A biscuit cake given to one, that one breaks it equally into so many parts as there be persons in his company, and distributes it. Plato's commonwealth is so much practiced by these people.

According to human reason, guided only by the light of nature, these people lead the more happy and freer life, being void of care, which torments the minds of so many Christians: They are not delighted in baubles, but in useful things. . . .

I have observed that they will not be troubled with superfluous commodities. Such things as they find they are taught by necessity to make use of, they will make choice of, and seek to purchase with industry. So that, in respect that their life is so void of care, and they are so loving also that they make use of those things they enjoy, (the wife only excepted) as common goods, and are therein so compassionate that, rather than one should starve through want, they would starve all. Thus do they pass away the time merrily, not regarding our pomp (which they see daily before their faces,) but are better content with their own, which some men esteem so meanly of.

The Indians Trust the English

William Wood

Like many early English accounts of colonists' interactions with the Indians, William Wood's description of Native Americans is largely genial and benign, as though intended to assuage his audience's preconceptions and prejudices. To a certain extent such was his design, since Wood seems to have composed his account in 1639 at the behest of Puritans in England. He had been granted permission by the colonial governor to trade with the indigenous peoples, and his account makes obvious his firsthand conviction of the trustworthiness of those with whom he dealt.

It is important to note, however, the distinction Wood draws between the New England Indians and more hostile, treacherous tribes. The book from which the following selection is taken was written in 1634, though published five years later; already the colonists had experienced decidedly mixed relations with the Native Americans. The initial peace treaty struck by the pilgrims with Massasoit had withered, culminating in the Pequot War of 1636–1638. However, little of the tension between the colonists and Indians finds its way into Wood's narrative.

As you read, consider the following questions:
1. What assumptions and preconceptions does Wood believe his English readers might have about Native Americans? Describe the tone Wood employs to address these preconceptions.
2. What, according to Wood, makes the Indians he describes more hospitable to Englishmen as opposed to

Excerpted from *New England's Prospect: A True, Lively, and Experimental Description of That Part of America,* by William Wood (London: John Dawson, 1639).

Spaniards or Frenchmen? Can you identify any of the contemporary English stereotypes Wood draws upon not only about the Indians, but also about non-English Europeans?

3. How might the Indians described here have seen Wood and other European colonists? What does the text indicate about their perspectives toward the settlers?

To enter into a serious discourse concerning the natural conditions of these Indians might procure admiration from the people of any civilized nations, in regard of their civility and good natures. If a tree may be judged by his fruit, and dispositions calculated by exterior actions, then may it be concluded that these Indians are of affable, courteous, and well-disposed natures, ready to communicate the best of their wealth to the mutual good of one another; . . .

Good Will Toward the English

If it were possible to recount the courtesies they have showed the English since their first arrival in those parts, it would not only steady belief that they are a loving people, but also win the love of those that never saw them, and wipe off that needless fear that is too deeply rooted in the conceits of many who think them envious and of such rancorous and inhumane dispositions that they will one day make an end of their English inmates. The worst indeed may be surmised, but the English hitherto have had little cause to suspect them but rather to be convinced of their trustiness, seeing they have as yet been the disclosers of all such treacheries as have been practiced by other Indians. And whereas once there was a proffer of an universal league amongst all the Indians in those parts, to the intent that they might all join in one united force to extirpate the English, our Indians refused the motion, replying they had rather be servants to the English, of whom they were confident to receive no harm and from whom they had received so many favors and assured good testimonies of their love, than equals with them who would cut their throats upon the least offence and make them the shambles of their cruelty.

An Advantageous Friendship

Furthermore, if any roving ships be upon the coasts and chance to harbor either eastward, northward, or southward in any unusual port, they will give us certain intelligence of her burden and forces, describing their men either by language or features, which is a great privilege and no small advantage. Many ways hath their advice and endeavor been advantageous unto us, they being our first instructors for the planting of their Indian corn, by teaching us to cull out the finest seed, to observe the fittest season, to keep distance for holes and fit measure for hills, to worm it and weed it, to prune it and dress it as occasion shall require. . . .

Such is the wisdom and policy of these poor men that they will be sure to keep correspondence with our English magistrates, expressing their love in the execution of any service they command them (so far as lies in their power). . . .

These people be of a kind and affable disposition, yet are they very wary with whom they strike hands in friendship. Nothing is more hateful to them than a churlish disposition, so likewise is dissimulation; he that speaks seldom and opportunely, being as good as his word, is the only man they love. The Spaniard they say is all one aramouse (viz., all one as a dog); the Frenchman hath a good tongue but a false heart; the Englishman all one speak, all one heart, wherefore they more approve of them than of any nation. Garrulity is much condemned of them, for they utter not many words, speak seldom, and then with such gravity as is pleasing to the ear. Such as understand them not desire yet to hear their emphatical expressions and lively action.

An Indian Attack

Mary Rowlandson

The peaceful relations between the colonists of New England and the various Native American tribes were undercut with tensions often belied by the somewhat idyllic (if condescending) accounts of early settlers. The Pequot War of 1637 was fierce but short-lived. King Philip's War, which broke out in the fall of 1675, was the bloodiest conflict between the colonists and the Indians. In many ways the culmination of decades of English colonial prosperity at the expense of the native tribes of New England, the war was instigated largely by Metacom (mockingly nicknamed "King Philip" by the Puritans due to his regal bearing), son of Massosoit, the Wampanoag chief who had been so helpful to the pilgrims. The Wampanoags and Nipmucks launched a series of attacks involving several tribes on settlements throughout southern New England, burning towns, killing settlers, and taking captives. The settlers bore heavy losses, and turned on the peaceful Narragansett Indians, massacring more than five hundred, mostly women and children. The Narragansetts joined the alliance against the colonists. It was only when the English attacked the major Wampanoag-Nipmuck camp along the Connecticut River, decimating the Indian ranks and fragmenting the alliance, that the tide began to turn in the colonists' favor. The beleaguered warriors continued sporadic raids, but in the summer of 1676 Metacom was shot to death by the Indian guide of Benjamin Church, which effectively ended the war.

Mary Rowlandson, a minister's wife, was taken captive with her three children by King Philip's warriors in February of 1676, during a raid on Lancaster [part of the Massachusetts Bay Colony]. She was held for six weeks before be-

Excerpted from *A True History of the Captivity and Restoration of Mrs. Mary Rowlandson, a Minister's Wife in New-England,* by Mary Rowlandson (London: Joseph Poole, 1682).

ing ransomed. Her account, published in 1682, was widely popular, not the least for the Christian providential perspective of the narrator herself. In the following excerpt, Rowlandson describes the brutal attack on Lancaster that resulted in her kidnapping.

As you read, consider the following questions:
1. Rowlandson characterizes the attack in religious as well as Eurocentric terms: "barbaric heathens" assailing "civilized" Christians. How does her account compare and contrast with earlier views of the Native Americans?
2. Rowlandson wrote her account retrospectively, after her release. How does her narrative reflect the fact that she is writing with the hindsight of having survived her ordeal?
3. The author admits that before the attack she had always believed she would rather die than be taken captive. What factors do you imagine changed her mind?

On the tenth of February 1675, came the Indians with great numbers upon Lancaster: their first coming was about sunrising; hearing the noise of some guns, we looked out; several houses were burning, and the smoke ascending to heaven. There were five persons taken in one house; the father, and the mother and a sucking child, they knocked on the head; the other two they took and carried away alive. There were two others, who being out of their garrison upon some occasion were set upon; one was knocked on the head, the other escaped; another there was who running along was shot and wounded, and fell down; he begged of them his life, promising them money (as they told me) but they would not hearken to him but knocked him in head, and stripped him naked, and split open his bowels. Another, seeing many of the Indians about his barn, ventured and went out, but was quickly shot down. There were three others belonging to the same garrison who were killed; the Indians getting up upon the roof of the barn, had advantage to shoot down upon them over their fortification. Thus these murderous wretches went on, burning, and destroying before them.

At length they came and beset our own house, and quickly it was the dolefulest day that ever mine eyes saw. The house stood upon the edge of a hill; some of the Indians got behind the hill, others into the barn, and others behind anything that could shelter them; from all which places they shot against the house, so that the bullets seemed to fly like hail; and quickly they wounded one man among us, then another, and then a third. About two hours (according to my observation, in that amazing time) they had been about the house before they prevailed to fire it (which they did with flax and hemp, which they brought out of the barn, and there being no defense about the house, only two flankers at two opposite corners and one of them not finished); they fired it once and one ventured out and quenched it, but they quickly fired it again, and that took. Now is the dreadful hour come, that I have often heard of (in time of war, as it was the case of others), but now mine eyes see it. Some in our house were fighting for their lives, others wallowing in their blood, the house on fire over our heads, and the bloody heathen ready to knock us on the head, if we stirred out. Now might we hear mothers and children crying out for themselves, and one another, "Lord, what shall we do?"

Rowlandson Attempts to Escape

Then I took my children (and one of my sisters', hers) to go forth and leave the house: but as soon as we came to the door and appeared, the Indians shot so thick that the bullets rattled against the house, as if one had taken an handful of stones and threw them, so that we were fain to give back. We had six stout dogs belonging to our garrison, but none of them would stir, though another time, if any Indian had come to the door, they were ready to fly upon him and tear him down. The Lord hereby would make us the more acknowledge His hand, and to see that our help is always in Him. But out we must go, the fire increasing, and coming along behind us, roaring, and the Indians gaping before us with their guns, spears, and hatchets to devour us.

No sooner were we out of the house, but my brother-in-law (being before wounded, in defending the house, in or near the throat) fell down dead, whereat the Indians scornfully shouted, and hallowed, and were presently upon him, stripping off his clothes, the bullets flying thick, one went through my side, and the same (as would seem) through the bowels and hand of my dear child in my arms. One of my elder sisters' children, named William, had then his leg broken, which the Indians perceiving, they knocked him on [his] head.

Thus were we butchered by those merciless heathen, standing amazed, with the blood running down to our heels. My eldest sister being yet in the house, and seeing those woeful sights, the infidels hauling mothers one way, and children another, and some wallowing in their blood: and her elder son telling her that her son William was dead, and myself was wounded, she said, "And Lord, let me die with them," which was no sooner said, but she was struck with a bullet, and fell down dead over the threshold. I hope she is reaping the fruit of her good labors, being faithful to the service of God in her place. In her younger years she lay under much trouble upon spiritual accounts, till it pleased God to make that precious scripture take hold of her heart, "And he said unto me, my Grace is sufficient for thee" (2 Corinthians 12.9). More than twenty years after, I have heard her tell how sweet and comfortable that place was to her.

Rowlandson Is Captured

But to return: the Indians laid hold of us, pulling me one way, and the children another, and said, "Come go along with us"; I told them they would kill me: they answered, if I were willing to go along with them, they would not hurt me.

Oh the doleful sight that now was to behold at this house! "Come, behold the works of the Lord, what desolations he has made in the earth." Of thirty-seven persons who were in this one house, none escaped either present death, or a bitter captivity, save only one, who might say as he, "And I only am escaped alone to tell the News" (Job 1.15). There were twelve killed, some shot, some stabbed with their spears, some knocked down with their hatchets. When we are in prosperity, Oh the little that we think of such dreadful sights, and to see our dear friends, and relations lie bleeding out their heart-blood upon the ground. There was one who was chopped into the head with a hatchet, and stripped naked, and yet was crawling up and down. It is a solemn sight to see so many Christians lying in their blood, some here, and some there, like a company of sheep torn by wolves, all of them stripped naked by a company of hell-hounds, roaring, singing, ranting, and insulting, as if they would have torn our very hearts out; yet the Lord by His almighty power preserved a number of us from death, for there were twenty-four of us taken alive and carried captive.

I had often before this said that if the Indians should come, I should choose rather to be killed by them than taken alive, but when it came to the trial my mind changed; their glittering weapons so daunted my spirit, that I chose rather to go along with those (as I may say) ravenous beasts, than that moment to end my days; and that I may the better declare what happened to me during that grievous captivity, I shall particularly speak of the several removes we had up and down the wilderness.

The Indians Bear Her Away

Now away we must go with those barbarous creatures, with our bodies wounded and bleeding, and our hearts no less than our bodies. About a mile we went that night, up upon a hill within sight of the town, where they intended to lodge. There was hard by a vacant house (deserted by the English before, for fear of the Indians). I asked them whether I might not lodge in the house that night, to which they answered, "What, will you love English men still?" This was the dolefulest night that ever my eyes saw. Oh the roaring, and singing and dancing, and yelling of those black creatures in the night, which made the place a lively resemblance of hell. And as miserable was the waste that was there made of horses, cattle, sheep, swine, calves, lambs, roasting pigs, and fowl (which they had plundered in the town), some roasting, some lying and burning, and some boiling to feed our merciless enemies; who were joyful enough, though we were disconsolate. To add to the dolefulness of the former day, and the dismalness of the present night, my thoughts ran upon my losses and sad bereaved condition. All was gone, my husband gone (at least separated from me, he being in the Bay; and to add to my grief, the Indians told me they would kill him as he came homeward), my children gone, my relations and friends gone, our house and home and all our comforts—within door and without—all was gone (except my life), and I knew not but the next moment that might go too. There remained nothing to me but one poor wounded babe, and it seemed at present worse than death that it was in such a pitiful condition, bespeaking compassion, and I had no refreshing for it, nor suitable things to revive it. Little do many think what is the savageness and brutishness of this barbarous enemy, Ay, even those that seem to profess more than others among them, when the English have fallen into their hands.

3

THE DARKER SIDE OF COLONIAL LIFE

CHAPTER PREFACE

Early colonial American life was marked by violence, prejudice, and destructiveness often born of the attempts to impose a rigid, racist social hierarchy on a land and culture at times frighteningly alien to the settlers. Most of the cultural ills imported by the colonists were by-products of the white patriarchal value system that dominated Europe. In England, sermons and secular literature alike preached a strict hierarchical view of the universe and those who inhabited it, with God at the summit and the rest of creation falling into prescribed places beneath. Even a minor challenge to this divinely ordained order could be viewed as disruptive to the entire macrocosm. In practice, this ideology worked to justify not only tyranny but also racism, sexism, and oppression of the disempowered. It also promoted the economic aims of the emerging colonial planter class, which needed virtual armies of cheap labor to harvest tobacco and perform other varieties of manual work. The first shipment of Virginia tobacco was exported in 1614; not coincidentally, the first twenty Africans, enslaved to be sold as indentured servants, arrived in the colonies five years later.

The Salem witch trials were similarly informed by Puritan sexual and religious prejudice, although they also came to include men in their destructive scope. The first person charged with witchcraft was Tituba, the Parris family's black slave from "heathen" Barbados. Although many seventeenth-century European intellectuals such as Sir Francis Bacon were starting to challenge the medieval belief in witches and demons, the Puritans in America remained largely convinced of the reality of supernatural, malevolent beings in their midst. The possible causes for the witch scare are still the subject of much scholarly conjecture. Certainly many colonial Puritans harbored a mistrust not only of the "heathen" religious practices of Indians, many of which were enslaved as domestic servants after the 1637 Pequot War, but also of such unorthodox Christian sects as the Quakers. The Massachusetts Bay Colony itself had endured over a decade of instability: A 1675 conflict with the Indians devastated the New England populace; King James had revoked the Massachusetts charter in 1685; when William III restored the charter in 1689, the colony was required to observe religious tolerance for non-Puritan Christians and to abolish religious criteria for voting. Moreover, local conflict between Salem Town and Salem Village exacerbated tensions in the colony, contributing to an atmosphere of paranoia and persecution. Lastly, adolescent mass hysteria originating in the fertile imaginations of the initial accusers may also have been a catalyst for the persecutions.

The Benefits of Indentured Servitude

John Hammond

The early colonists expected to find their fortunes in the new land through discovery of precious metals, but within the first decade of the Virginia Company's establishment it became evident that planting—especially of tobacco—and farming were to be the chief form of revenue. The settlers thus required a large workforce of manual laborers, for which they engaged indentured servants—men whose passage to the New World was paid for by wealthy colonists with the understanding that the new arrival would work for the sponsor to pay off this debt. (Indentured servants would also come to serve in menial trade and domestic capacities as well).

The system of indentured servitude first appeared in Virginia in the second decade of the 1600s. Servants were generally drawn from the classes of paupers, debtors, and criminals, some petty and some serious felons. In England a term of servitude, sealed by an "indenture" or contract between the parties, usually lasted from two to three years, but in the colonies the term more often ranged from four to seven. The system was unquestionably exploitative; many servants were physically abused and subjected to inhumane living conditions. Runaways were punished harshly if apprehended. But advocates argued that servitude was not only benign but beneficial, promoting Puritan virtues of industriousness and morality while providing the laborers with not only bed and board, but a viable trade to play once the term of indenture expired.

The following selection, written by pamphleteer John Hammond in 1656, begins by condemning the moral laxity

Excerpted from *Leah and Rachel, or, The Two Fruitful Sisters Virginia and Mary-Land: Their Present Condition, Impartially Stated and Related*, by John Hammond (Virginia, 1656).

of early Virginia experiments in indentured servitude, which he claimed mistreated servants, fostered vice and infested the colony with sordid personages. But Hammond argues that the practice has since been reformed, and characterizes it as a species of apprenticeship, wherein the laborer is ultimately rewarded for his or her indenture with a marketable skill and often provisions and a parcel of land. Overall, he describes a rigorous but reasonable labor system, though anecdotal evidence contradicts his rather indulgent perspective.

As you read, consider the following questions:

1. What are the safeguards Hammond sees as in place to deter abuse of indentured servitude? What may these safeguards tell us about his beliefs concerning master-servant relationships?
2. Hammond implies a comparison between indentured servitude and African slavery. To what extent might his reasons justifying servitude also be applied to slavery?
3. From Hammond's description, one might infer that indentured servitude is not greatly more exploitative than the apprenticeship system, as both seem to provide the servant with room, board, and a trade by which to make a living later. What are some key distinctions, however, between the two systems?

It is the glory of every Nation to enlarge themselves, to encourage their own foreign attempts, and to be able to have their own, within their territories, as many several commodities as they can attain to, that so others may rather be beholding to them, than they to others. . . . But alas, we Englishmen . . . do not only fail in this, but vilify, scandalize and cry down such parts of the unknown world, as have been found out, settled and made flourishing, by the charge, hazard, and diligence of their own brethren, as if because removed from us, we either account them people of another world or enemies. This is too truly made good in the odious and cruel slanders cast on those two famous countries of Virginia and Mary-land, whereby those countries, not only are many times at a stand, but are in danger to molder away, and come in time to nothing. . . .

The country [Virginia] is reported to be an unhealthy place, a nest of rogues, whores, dissolute and rooking persons; a place of intolerable labour, bad usage and hard diet, &c. To answer these several calumnies, I shall first show what it was? Next, what it is? At the first settling and many years after, it deserved most of those aspersions (nor were they aspersions but truths). . . . Then were Jails emptied, youth seduced, infamous women drilled in, the provisions all brought out of England, and that embezzled by the trustees (for they durst neither hunt fowl, nor fish, for fear of the Indian, which they stood in awe of) their labour was almost perpetual, their allowance of victual small, few or no cattle, no use of horses nor oxen to draw or carry, (which labours men supplied themselves) all of which caused a mortality; no civil courts of justice but under a martial law, no redress of grievances, complaints were repaid with stripes [whippings] . . . in a word all and the worst that tyranny could inflict. . . . And having briefly laid down the former state of Virginia, in its infancy, and filth, and the occasion of its scandalous aspersions: I come to my main subject, its present condition of happiness (if anything can be called happy in this transitory life). . . .

The Terms of Servitude
The usual allowance for servants is (besides their charge of passage defrayed) at their expiration, a year's provision of corn, double apparel, tools necessary, and land according to the custom of the country, which is an old delusion, for there is no land customarily due to the servant, but to the master, and therefore that servant is unwise that will not dash out that custom in his covenant and make that due of land absolutely his own, which although at the present, not of so great consequences; yet in few years will be of much worth. : . . . When ye go aboard, expect the ship somewhat

troubled and in a hurlyburly, until ye clear the lands end; and that the ship is rummaged, and things put to rights, which many times discourages the passengers, and makes them wish the voyage unattempted: but this is but for a short season, and washes off when at sea, where the time is pleasantly passed away, though not with such choice plenty as the shore affords. But when ye arrive and are settled, ye will find a strange alteration, an abused country giving the lie to your own approbations to those that have calumniated it. . . . The labour servants are put to, is not so hard nor of such continuance as husbandmen [herders], nor handicraftmen are kept at in England, I said little or nothing is done in winter time, none ever work before sun rising nor after sun set, in the summer they rest, sleep or exercise themselves give hours in the heat of the day, Saturdays afternoon is always their own, the old holidays are observed and the Sabbath spent in good exercises. The women are not (as is reported) put into the ground to work, but occupy such domestic employments and housewifery as in England, that is dressing victuals, right up the house, milking, employed about dairies, washing, sewing, &c. and both men and women have times of recreations, as much or more than in any part of the world besides, yet some wenches that are nastily, beastly and not fit to be so employed are put into the ground, for reason tells us, they must not at charge be transported then maintained for nothing, but those that prove so awkward are rather burthensome than servants desirable or useful. . . .

Those servants that will be industrious may in their time of service gain a competent estate before their freedoms, which is usually done by many, and they gain esteem and assistance that appear so industrious: There is no master almost but will allow his servant a parcel of clear ground to cut some tobacco in for himself, which he may husband at those many idle times he hath allowed him and not prejudice, but rejoice his master to see it, which in time of shipping he may lay out for commodities, and in summer sell them again with advantage and get a pig or two, which any body almost will give him, and his master suffer him to keep them with his own, which will be no charge to his master, and with one years increase of them may purchase a cow calf or two, and by that time he is for himself; he may have cattle, hogs and tobacco of his own, and come to live gallantly; but this must be gained (as I have said) by industry and affability, not by sloth nor churlish behavior.

The Servants' Living Condition

And whereas it is rumoured that servants have no lodgings other then on boards, or by the fire side, it is contrary to reason to believe it: First, as we are Christians; next as people living under a law, which compels as well the master as the servant to perform his duty; nor can true labour be either expected or exacted without sufficient clothing, diet, and lodging; all which their indentures (which must inviolably be observed) and the justice of the country requires. But if any go thither, not in a condition of a servant, but pay his or her passage, which is some six pounds: Let them not doubt but it is money well laid out . . . although they carry little else to take a bed along with them, and then few houses but will give them entertainment, either out of courtesy, or on reasonable terms; and I think it better for any that goes over free, and but in a mean condition, to hire himself for reasonable wages of tobacco and provision, the first year, provided he happen in an honest house, and where the mistress is noted for a good housewife, of which there are very many (notwithstanding the cry to the contrary) for by that means he will live free of disbursement, have something to help him the next year, and be carefully looked to in his sickness (if he chance to fall sick) and let him so covenant that exceptions may be made, that he work not much in the hot weather, a course we always take with our new hands (as they call them) the first year they come in. If they are women that go after this manner, that is paying their own passages; I advise them to sojourn in a house of honest repute, for by their good carriage, they may advance themselves in marriage, by their ill, overthrow their

fortunes; and although loose persons seldom live long unmarried if free; yet they match with as dissolute as themselves, and never live handsomely or are ever respected. . . .

Be sure to have your contract in writing and under hand
and seal, for if ye go over upon promise made to do this or
that, or to be free, it signifies nothing.

The Misfortunes of Indentured Servants

Gottlieb Mittelberger

Indentured servitude continued to provide a relatively inexpensive source of labor for the colonies, and in fact, was not outlawed in America until 1885. Some historians have speculated that as many as one-third to one-half of colonial immigrants arrived under indentures. The original predominance of criminal servants soon swelled to include poor Protestant families from Germany and the Netherlands seeking religious refuge, known as "redemptioners" for their willingness to exchange terms of servitude for the cost of passage to America.

But throughout the eighteenth and nineteenth centuries indentured servitude became less common, as it gradually gave way to slavery. The reasons for its decline were both economic and moral: Unlike indentured servitude, slavery was perpetual; the qualms held by some Christians about virtually enslaving their fellow white men and women; and the increasing affordability of passage to the colonies, which served to shrink the pool of laborers willing to sign indenture contracts. The following account of the arduous voyage and dismal future of indentured servants, written by schoolteacher and emigrant Gottlieb Mittelberger, demonstrates not only how commonplace indentured servitude still was in 1750, but also a heightened concern about the humaneness of such a system.

As you read, consider the following questions:
1. Mittelberger especially focuses on the toll servitude exacts on families. What does this emphasis perhaps suggest

Excerpted from *Journey to Pennsylvania in the Year 1750*, by Gottlieb Mittelberger, translated by Carl Theo (Philadelphia: John Joseph McVey, 1898).

about a connection between humanitarian concern and the social status of the prospective servants? Do you imagine the same concern was extended to convict immigrants?

2. Explain the connection Mittelberger makes between shipboard conditions and the fates of the passengers once ashore. Why do you think he does not seem to argue simply for improving the former?

3. Analyze how Mittelberger's word choice and narrative structure contribute to the power of his account. What are the responses the author must have intended to provoke in his reader?

Both in Rotterdam and in Amsterdam the people are packed densely, like herrings so to say, in the large sea-vessels. One person receives a place of scarcely 2 feet width and 6 feet length in the bedstead, while many a ship carries four to six hundred souls; not to mention the innumerable implements, tools, provisions, water-barrels and other things which likewise occupy much space.

On account of contrary winds it takes the ships sometimes 2, 3 and 4 weeks to make the trip from Holland to . . . England. But when the wind is good, they get there in 8 days or even sooner. Everything is examined there and the custom-duties paid, whence it comes that the ships ride there 8, 10 to 14 days and even longer at anchor, till they have taken in their full cargoes. During that time every one is compelled to spend his last remaining money and to consume his little stock of provisions which had been reserved for the sea; so that most passengers, finding themselves on the ocean where they would be in greater need of them, must greatly suffer from hunger and want. Many suffer want already on the water between Holland and Old England.

An Arduous Journey
When the ships have for the last time weighed their anchors near the city of Kaupp [Cowes] in Old England, the real misery begins with the long voyage. For from there the

ships, unless they have good wind, must often sail 8, 9, 10 to 12 weeks before they reach Philadelphia. But even with the best wind the voyage lasts 7 weeks.

But during the voyage there is on board these ships terrible misery, stench, fumes, horror, vomiting, many kinds of sea-sickness, fever, dysentery, headache, heat, constipation, boils, scurvy, cancer, mouth-rot, and the like, all of which come from old and sharply salted food and meat, also from very bad and foul water, so that many die miserably.

Add to this want of provisions, hunger, thirst, frost, heat, dampness, anxiety, want, afflictions and lamentations, together with other trouble, as . . . the lice abound so frightfully, especially on sick people, that they can be scraped off the body. The misery reaches the climax when a gale rages for 2 or 3 nights and days, so that every one believes that the ship will go to the bottom with all human beings on board. In such a visitation the people cry and pray most piteously.

When in such a gale the sea rages and surges, so that the waves rise often like high mountains one above the other, and often tumble over the ship, so that one fears to go down with the ship; when the ship is constantly tossed from side to side by the storm and waves, so that no one can either walk, or sit, or lie, and the closely packed people in the berths are thereby tumbled over each other, both the sick and the well—it will be readily understood that many of these people, none of whom had been prepared for hardships, suffer so terribly from them that they do not survive it.

The Travails of Immigrant Families

I myself had to pass through a severe illness at sea, and I best know how I felt at the time. These poor people often long for consolation, and I often entertained and comforted them with singing, praying and exhorting; and whenever it was possible and the winds and waves permitted it, I kept daily prayer-meetings with them on deck. Besides, I baptized five children in distress, because we had no ordained minister on board. I also held divine service every

Sunday by reading sermons to the people; and when the dead were sunk in the water, I commended them and our souls to the mercy of God.

Among the healthy, impatience sometimes grows so great and cruel that one curses the other, or himself and the day of his birth, and sometimes come near killing each other. Misery and malice join each other, so that they cheat and rob one another. One always reproaches the other with having persuaded him to undertake the journey. Frequently children cry out against their parents, husbands against their wives and wives against their husbands, brothers and sisters, friends and acquaintances against each other. But most against the soul-traffickers.

Many sigh and cry: "Oh, that I were at home again, and if I had to lie in my pig-sty!" Or they say: "O God, if I only had a piece of good bread, or a good fresh drop of water." Many people whimper, sigh and cry piteously for their homes; most of them get home-sick. Many hundred people necessarily die and perish in such misery, and must be cast into the sea, which drives their relatives, or those who persuaded them to undertake the journey, to such despair that it is almost impossible to pacify and console them.

No one can have an idea of the sufferings which women in confinement have to bear with their innocent children on board these ships. Few of this class escape with their lives; many a mother is cast into the water with her child as soon as she is dead. One day, just as we had a heavy gale, a woman in our ship, who was to give birth and could not give birth under the circumstances, was pushed through a loop-hole [port-hole] in the ship and dropped into the sea, because she was far in the rear of the ship and could not be brought forward.

Children from 1 to 7 years rarely survive the voyage. I witnessed misery in no less than 32 children in our ship, all of whom were thrown into the sea. The parents grieve all the more since their children find no resting-place in the earth, but are devoured by the monsters of the sea.

That most of the people get sick is not surprising, because, in addition to all other trials and hardships, warm food is served only three times a week, the rations being very poor and very little. Such meals can hardly be eaten, on account of being so unclean. The water which is served out on the ships is often very black, thick and full of worms, so that one cannot drink it without loathing, even with the greatest thirst. Toward the end we were compelled to eat the ship's biscuit which had been spoiled long ago; though in a whole biscuit there was scarcely a piece the size of a dollar that had not been full of red worms and spiders nests.

Approaching Land

At length, when, after a long and tedious voyage, the ships come in sight of land, so that the promontories can be seen, which the people were so eager and anxious to see, all creep from below on deck to see the land from afar, and they weep for joy, and pray and sing, thanking and praising God. The sight of the land makes the people on board the ship, especially the sick and the half dead, alive again, so that their hearts leap within them; they shout and rejoice, and are content to bear their misery in patience, in the hope that they may soon reach the land in safety. But alas!

When the ships have landed at Philadelphia after their long voyage, no one is permitted to leave them except those who pay for their passage or can give good security; the others, who cannot pay, must remain on board the ships till they are purchased, and are released from the ships by their purchasers. The sick always fare the worst, for the healthy are naturally preferred and purchased first; and so the sick and wretched must often remain on board in front of the city for 2 or 3 weeks, and frequently die, whereas many a one, if he could pay his debt and were permitted to leave the ship immediately, might recover and remain alive.

The Sale of Servants

The sale of human beings in the market on board the ship is carried on thus: Every day Englishmen, Dutchmen and High-German people come from the city of Philadelphia and other places, in part from a great distance, say 20, 30, or 40 hours away, and go on board the newly arrived ship that has brought and offers for sale passengers from Europe, and select among the healthy persons such as they deem suitable for their business, and bargain with them how long they will serve for their passage money, which most of them are still in debt for. When they have come to an agreement, it happens that adult persons bind themselves in writing to serve 3, 4, 5 or 6 years for the amount due by them, according to their age and strength. But very young people, from 10 to 15 years, must serve till they are 21 years old.

Many parents must sell and trade away their children like so many head of cattle; for if their children take the debt upon themselves, the parents can leave the ship free and unrestrained; but as the parents often do not know where and to what people their children are going, it often happens that such parents and children, after leaving the ship, do not see each other again for many years, perhaps no more in all their lives.

It often happens that whole families, husband, wife, and children, are separated by being sold to different purchasers, especially when they have not paid any part of their passage money.

When a husband or wife has died at sea, when the ship has made more than half of her trip, the survivor must pay or serve not only for himself or herself, but also for the deceased.

When both parents have died over half-way at sea, their children, especially when they are young and have nothing to pawn or to pay, must stand for their own and their parents' passage, and serve till they are 21 years old. When one has served his or her term, he or she is entitled to a new suit of clothes at parting; and if it has been so stipulated, a man gets in addition a horse, a woman, a cow.

When a serf has an opportunity to marry in this country, he or she must pay for each year which he or she would have yet to serve, 5 to 6 pounds. But many a one who has thus purchased and paid for his bride, has subsequently re-pented his bargain, so that he would gladly have returned his exorbitantly dear ware, and lost the money besides.

If some one in this country runs away from his master, who has treated him harshly, he cannot get far. Good provision has been made for such cases, so that a runaway is soon recovered. He who detains or returns a deserter receives a good reward.

If such a runaway has been away from his master one day, he must serve for it as a punishment a week, for a week a month, and for a month half a year.

An Exhortation Against Buying and Keeping Slaves

George Keith

By the second half of the seventeenth century, African slavery was becoming increasingly entrenched in the colonies. Its benefits, especially to planters in the southern colonies, were obvious; unlike indentured servitude, slavery was perpetual, and racial prejudice worked to justify the subjection of a nonwhite, non-Christian people, who, unlike the Indians, were far removed from their native communities that might have sought to rescue them. The transatlantic slave trade flourished, providing a steady supply of cheap labor to the colonies, often by way of the Caribbean.

Abolitionism, as a movement, would not emerge until the American Revolution, and it remained a marginalized, sectionalist cause until the Civil War. But that is not to say that all colonial Americans accepted unquestioningly the justice of slavery. The following document, written by Quaker radical George Keith in 1693, was the first antislavery tract to appear in the colonies. Keith was a prolific advocate for Quaker doctrine as well as the first headmaster of the Quaker School in Philadelphia, author of over thirty books and tracts. Keith broke with the Friends to found the short-lived "Christian Quakers" in the 1690s, a splinter sect more closely focused on the life and teachings of Jesus Christ. In his treatise, he integrates Quaker ideals of social justice with citations of biblical authority to demonstrate the immorality of slavery and the duty of Christians to oppose it.

Excerpted from "The First Printed Protest Against Slavery in America," by George Keith, *The Pennsylvania Magazine of History and Biography*, 1889.

As you read, consider the following questions:

1. Would Keith's objections to slavery also apply to indentured servitude?
2. In what ways does Keith suggest that slavery is not only detrimental to the Christian's moral standing, but also to society as a whole?
3. How does the author's argument suggest to modern readers what must have been the common justifications for slavery?

Seeing our Lord Jesus Christ hath tasted death for every man, and given himself a ransom for all, to be testified in due time, and that his Gospel of peace, liberty and redemption from sin, bondage and all oppression, is freely to be preached unto all, without exception, and that Negroes, Blacks, and Taunies ["Tawnies," presumably Indians] are a real part of mankind, for whom Christ hath shed his precious blood, and are capable of salvation, as well as white men; and Christ the Light of the World hath (in measure) enlightened them, and every man that cometh into the world; and that all such who are sincere Christians and true believers in Christ Jesus, and followers of him, bear his Image, and are made conformable unto him in love, mercy, goodness and compassion, who came not to destroy men's lives, but to save them, nor to bring any part of mankind into outward bondage, slavery or misery, nor yet to detain them, or hold them therein, but to ease and deliver the oppressed and distressed, and bring into liberty both inward and outward.

Therefore we judge it necessary that all faithful Friends should discover themselves to be true Christians by having the fruits of the Spirit of Christ, which are love, mercy, goodness, and compassion towards all in misery, and that suffer oppression and severe usage, so far as in them is possible to ease and relieve them, and set them free of their hard bondage, whereby it may be hoped, that many of them will be gained by their beholding these good works of sincere Christians, and prepared thereby, through the preaching the Gospel of Christ, to imbrace the true Faith of Christ. And for this cause it is, as we judge, that in some places in Europe Negroes cannot be bought and sold for money, or detained to be slaves, because it suits not with the mercy, love & clemency that is essential to Christianity, nor to the doctrine of Christ, nor to the liberty the Gospel calleth all men unto, to whom it is preached. And to buy souls and bodies of men for money, to enslave them and their posterity to the end of the world, we judge is a great hindrance to the spreading of the Gospel, and is occasion of much war, violence, cruelty and oppression, and theft & robbery of the highest nature; for commonly the Negroes that are sold to white men, are either stolen away or robbed from their kindred, and to buy such is the way to continue these evil practices of man-stealing, and transgresseth that Golden Rule and Law, To do to others what we would have others do to us.

Slavery Is Un-Christian

Therefore, in true Christian love, we earnestly recommend it to all our Friends and brethren, not to buy any Negroes, unless it were on purpose to set them free, and that such who have bought any, and have them at present, after some reasonable time of moderate service they have had of them, or may have of them, that may reasonably answer to the charge of what they have laid out, especially in keeping Negroes' children born in their house, or taken into their house, when under age, that after a reasonable time of service to answer that charge, they may set them at liberty, and during the time they have them, to teach them to read, and give them a Christian education.

Some Reasons and Causes of Our Being Against Keeping Negroes

First, because it is contrary to the principles and practice of the Christian Quakers to buy prize or stolen goods, which we bore a faithful testimony against in our native country;

and therefore it is our duty to come forth in a testimony against stolen slaves, it being accounted a far greater crime under Moses's law than the stealing of goods: for such were only to restore four fold, but he that stealeth a man and selleth him, if he be found in his hand, he shall surely be put to death (Exod. 21. 16). Therefore as we are not to buy stolen goods, (but if at unawares it should happen through ignorance, we are to restore them to the owners; and seek our remedy of the thief) no more are we to buy stolen slaves; neither should such as have them keep them and their posterity in perpetual bondage and slavery, as is usually done, to the great scandal of the Christian profession.

Secondly, because Christ commanded, saying, All things whatsoever ye would that men should do unto you, do ye even so to them. Therefore as we and our children would not be kept in perpetual bondage and slavery against our consent, neither should we keep them in perpetual bondage and slavery against their consent, it being such intolerable punishment to their bodies and minds, that none but notorious criminal offendors deserve the same. But these have done us no harm; therefore how inhumane is it in us so grievously to oppress them and their children from one generation to another.

The Oppressed Must Be Protected

Thirdly, because the Lord hath commanded, saying, Thou shalt not deliver unto his master the servant that is escaped from his master unto thee, he shall dwell with thee, even amongst you in that place which he shall choose in one of thy gates, where it liketh him best; thou shalt oppress him (Deut. 23. 15. 16). By which it appeareth, that those which are at liberty and freed from their bondage, should not by us be delivered into bondage again, neither by us should they be oppressed, but being escaped from his master, should have the liberty to dwell amongst us, where it liketh him best. Therefore, if God extend such mercy under the legal ministration and dispensation to poor servants, he doth and will extend much more of his grace and mercy to them under the clear Gospel ministration; so that instead of punishing them and their posterity with cruel bondage and perpetual slavery, he will cause the everlasting Gospel to be preached effectually to all nations, to them as well as others; And the Lord will extend peace to his people like a river, and the glory of the gentiles like a flowing stream; And it shall come to pass, saith the Lord, that I will gather all nations and tongues, and they shall come and see my glory, and I will set a sign among them, and I will send those that escape of them unto the nations, to Tarshish, Pull and Lud that draw the bow to Tuball and Javan, to the isles afar off that have not heard my fame, neither have seen my glory, and they shall declare my glory among the Gentiles (Isa. 66. 12–18).

Fourthly, because the Lord hath commanded, saying, Thou shalt not oppress an hired servant that is poor and needy, whether he be of thy brethren, or of the strangers that are in thy land within thy gates, least he cry against thee unto the Lord, and it be sin unto thee; Thou shalt neither vex a stranger nor oppress him, for ye were strangers in the land of Egypt (Deut. 24. 14, 15). (Exod. 12. 21). But what greater oppression can there be inflicted upon our fellow creatures, than is inflicted on the poor Negroes! they being brought from their own country against their wills, some of them being stolen, others taken for payment of debt owing by their parents, and others taken captive in war, and sold to merchants, who bring them to the American plantations, and sell them for bond slaves to them that will give most for them; the husband from the wife, and the children from the parents; and many that buy them do exceedingly afflict them and oppress them, not only by continual hard labor, but by cruel whippings, and other cruel punishments, and by short allowance of food, some planters in Barbadoes and Jamaica, 'tis said, keeping one hundred of them, and some more, and some less, and giving them hardly any thing more than they raise on a little piece of ground appointed them, on which they work for themselves the seventh days of the week in the afternoon, and on the first days, to raise their own provisions, to wit, corn and potatoes, and other roots, &c. the remainder of their time being spent in their masters' service; which doubtless is far worse usage than is practised by the Turks and Moors upon their slaves. Which tends to the great reproach of the Christian Profession; therefore it would be better for all such as fall short of the practice of those infidels, to refuse the name of a Christian, that those heathen and infidels may not be provoked to blaspheme against the blessed name of Christ, by reason of the unparallel'd cruelty of these cruel and hard hearted pretended Christians: Surely the Lord doth behold their oppressions & afflictions, and will further visit for the same by his righteous and just judgments, except they break off their sins by repentance, and their iniquity by showing mercy to these poor afflicted, tormented miserable slaves!

The Judgment of God

Fifthly, because slaves and souls of men are some of the merchandise of Babylon by which the merchants of the earth are made rich; but those riches which they have heaped together, through the cruel oppression of these miserable creatures, will be a means to draw God's judgments upon them; therefore, brethren, let us hearken to the Voice of the Lord, who saith, come out of Babylon, my people, that ye be not partakers of her sins, and that ye receive not her plagues; for her sins have reached unto Heaven, and God hath remembered her iniquities; for he that leads into captivity shall go into captivity (Rev. 18. 4, 5. & 13. 10).

Given forth by our monthly meeting in Philadelphia, the 13th day of the 8th Month, 1693. and recommended to all our Friends and brethren, who are one with us in our testimony for the Lord Jesus Christ, and to all others professing Christianity.

Witches Should Be Condemned

Cotton Mather

Perhaps no colonial Puritan clergyman is better known than Cotton Mather (1662–1727). Indeed, in the popular imagination Mather has come to embody the overzealous, superstitious Puritan minister almost to the point of caricature. It is well to keep in mind that the Harvard-educated Mather hailed from a venerable line of Puritan theologians (the son of Increase Mather, his grandfathers were Richard Mather and John Cotton). He produced over 450 works of writing, and while his chief concerns, reflecting his background and education, focused on theological issues, he was also an early advocate of inoculation against smallpox and avidly interested in scientific and medical innovations.

Mather certainly played a key role in fueling the Salem witchcraft persecutions of 1692, but it is worth noting that the debate over the existence of witches and demons in early modern Europe counterpoised theologians and rationalists; there is no clear cutoff date marking the end of medieval beliefs in malevolent spiritual meddling in human affairs and the beginning of a more scientific understanding of reality. James I of England believed so strongly in witchcraft and demonology that he authored a book on the subject. Sir Robert Burton's vastly influential *Anatomy of Melancholy* (1622), however, reflected the growing view that supernatural phenomena originated not from demonic spirits but the individual disturbed psyche. Mather's views on witchcraft, expressed in the following sermon, were not atypical or unusually extreme among conservative-minded seventeenth-century Christians. In fact, Mather's positions

Excerpted from *Memorable Providences Relating to Witchcrafts and Possessions*, by Cotton Mather (Massachusetts, 1689).

were comparatively moderate, allowing as they do for repentance and redemption.

As you read, consider the following questions:
1. Consider the distinctions Mather draws between witchcraft and authentic miracles. Do you find his distinctions convincing?
2. Despite his denunciations of witchcraft in general, identify any instances in the selection where Mather seems to advocate pity or compassion for those possessed.
3. Compare Mather's language and tone with that of Jonathan Edwards. What similarities exist in their respective characterizations of the devil and God? What do these similarities suggest about the Puritan mind-set?

Proposition I

Such an Hellish thing there is as Witchcraft in the World. There are Two things which will be desired for the advantage of this Assertion. It should first be showed,

WHAT Witchcraft is.

My Hearers will not expect from me an accurate definition of the vile Thing; since the Grace of God has given me the Happiness to speak without Experience of it. But from Accounts both by Reading and Hearing I have learn'd to describe it so.

WITCHCRAFT is the doing of strange (and for the most part ill) things by the help of evil Spirits, covenanting with (and usually Representing of) the woeful Children of Men.

This is the Diabolical Art that Witches are notorious for.

First, Witches are the Doers of strange Things. They cannot indeed perform any proper Miracles; those are things to be done only by the Favorites and Ambassadors of the lord. But Wonders are often produced by them, though chiefly such Wonders as the Apostle calls in 2 Thes. 2. 9. Lying Wonders. There are wonderful Storms in the great World, and wonderful Wounds in the little World, often effected by these evil Causes. They do things which transcend the ordinary course of Nature, and which puzzle the ordinary Sense of Mankind. Some strange things are done by them in a way of Real Production. They do really Torment, they do really Afflict those that their Spite shall extend unto. Other strange things are done by them in a way of Crafty Illusion. They do craftily make of the Air, the Figures and Colors of things that never can be truly created by them. All men might see, but, I believe, no man could feel some of the Things which the Magicians of Egypt, exhibited of old.

Secondly, They are not only strange things, but ill things, that Witches are the Doers of. In this regard also they are not the Authors of Miracles: those are things commonly done for the good of Man, always done for the praise of god. But of these Hell-hounds it may in a special manner be said, as in Psal. 52. 3. Thou lovest evil more than good. For the most part they labor to rob Man of his Ease or his Wealth; they labor to wrong God of his Glory. There is mention of Creatures that they call White Witches, which do only Good-Turns for their Neighbors. I suspect that there are none of that sort; but rather think, There is none that doeth good no, not one. If they do good, it is only that they may do hurt.

The Aid of Evil Spirits

Thirdly, It is by virtue of evil Spirits that Witches do what they do. We read in Ephes. 22. about the Prince of the power of the Air. There is confined unto the Atmosphere of our Air a vast Power, or Army of Evil Spirits, under the Government of a Prince who employs them in a continual Opposition to the Designs of god: The Name of that Leviathan who is the Grand Seignior of Hell, we find in the Scripture to be Beelzebub. Under the Command of that mighty Tyrant, there are vast Legions and Myriads of Devils, whose businesses and accomplishments are not all the same. Every one has his Post, and his Work; and they are all glad of an opportunity to be mischievous in the World. These are they by whom Witches do exert their devilish and malignant rage upon their Neighbors: And especially Two

Acts concur hereunto. The First is, Their Covenanting with the Witches. There is a most hellish League made between them, with various Rites and Ceremonies. The Witches promise to serve the Devils, and the Devils promise to help the Witches; how? It is not convenient to be related. The Second is, Their Representing of the Witches. And hereby indeed these are drawn into Snares and Cords of Death. The Devils, when they go upon the Errands of the Witches, do bear their Names; and hence do Harms too come to be carried from the Devils to the Witches. We need not suppose such a wild thing as the Transforming of those Wretches into Brutes or Birds, as we too often do.

It should next be proved that Witchcraft is.

The Being of such a thing is denied by many that place a great part of their small wit in deriding the Stories that are told of it. Their chief Argument is, that they never saw any Witches, therefore there are none. Just as if you or I should say, we never met with any Robbers on the Road, therefore there was never any Padding there.

Indeed the Devils are loath to have true Notions of Witches entertained with us. I have beheld them to put out the Eyes of an Enchanted Child, when a Book that proves, There is Witchcraft, was laid before her. But there are especially two Demonstrations that Evince the Being of that Infernal mysterious thing.

Testimony as Proof

First, We have the Testimony of Scripture for it. We find Witchcrafts often mentioned, sometimes by way of Assertion, sometimes by way of Allusion, in the Oracles of God. Besides that, We have there the History of divers Witches in these infallible and inspired Writings. Particularly, the Instance of the Witch at Endor, in I Sam. 28. 7. is so plain and full that Witchcraft itself is not a more amazing thing than any Dispute about the Being of it, after this. The Advocates of Witches must use more Tricks to make Nonsense of the Bible, than ever the Witch of Endor used in her Magical Incantations, if they would Evade the Force of that Famous

History. They that will believe no Witches, do imagine that Jugglers only are meant by them whom the Sacred Writ calleth so. But what do they think of that Law in Exod. 22. 18. Thou shalt not suffer a Witch to live? Methinks 'tis a little too hard to punish every silly Juggler with so great severity.

Secondly, We have the Testimony of Experience for it. What will those Incredulous, who must be the only Ingenious Men say to this? Many Witches have like those in Acts 19. 18. Confessed and showed their Deeds. We see those things done, that it is impossible any Disease, or any Deceit should procure. We see some hideous Wretches in hideous Horrors confessing, That they did the Mischiefs. This Confession is often made by them that are owners of as much Reason as the people that laugh at all Conceit of Witchcraft: The Exactest Scrutiny of Skillful Physicians cannot find any distraction in their minds. This Confession is often made by them that are apart one from another, and yet they agree in all the Circumstances of it. This Confession is often made by them that at the same time will produce the Engines and Ensigns of their Hellish Trade, and give the standers-by an Ocular Conviction of what they do, and how. There can be no Judgment left of any Human Affairs, if such Confessions must be Ridiculed: all the Murders, yea, and all the Bargains in the World must be mere Imaginations if such Confessions are of no Account.

Proposition II

WITCHCRAFT is a most Monstrous and Horrid Evil. Indeed there is a vast Heap of Bloody Roaring Impieties contained in the Bowels of it. Witchcraft, is a Renouncing of God, and Advancing of a filthy Devil into the Throne of the Most High; 'tis the most nefandous High-Treason against the MAJESTY on High. Witchcraft, is a Renouncing of Christ, and preferring the Communion of a loathesome lying Devil before all the Salvation of the Lord Redeemer; 'tis a Trampling under foot that Blood which is more precious than Hills of Silver, or whole Mountains of Gold. There is in Witchcraft, a most explicit Renouncing of all that is

Holy, and Just and Good. The Law given by God, the Prayer taught by Christ, the Creed left by the Apostles, is become Abominable where Witchcraft is Embraced: The very Reciting of those blessed things is commonly burdensome where Witchcraft is. All the sure Mercies of the New Covenant, and all the just Duties of it, are utterly abdicated by that cursed Covenant which Witchcraft is Constituted with. Witchcraft is a Siding with Hell against Heaven and Earth; and therefore a Witch is not to be endured in either of them. 'Tis a Capital Crime; and it is to be prosecuted as a piece of Devilism that would not only deprive God and Christ of all His Honor, but also plunder Man of all his Comfort. Witchcraft, it's an impotent, but an impudent Essay to make an Hell of the Universe, and to allow Nothing but a Tophet in the World. Witchcraft,—What shall I say of it! It is the furthest Effort of our Original Sin; and all that can make any Practice or Persons odious, is here in the Exalt[at]ion of it. . . .

What We Must Do

II. By way of Exhortation.

There is one thing to be now pressed upon us all.

Let us wisely endeavor to be preserved from the Molestations of all Witchcraft whatsoever. Since there is a thing so dangerous, defend yourselves, and shelter yourselves by all right means against the annoyance of it.

Consider the Multitudes of them, whom Witchcraft hath sometimes given Trouble to. Persons of all sorts have been racked and ruined by it; and not a few of them neither. It is hardly twenty years ago; that a whole Kingdom in Europe was alarmed by such potent Witchcrafts, that some hundreds of poor Children were invaded with them. Persons of great Honor have sometimes been cruelly bewitched. What lately befell a worthy Knight in Scotland, is well known unto the World. Persons of great Virtue too have been bewitched, even into their Graves. But four years are passed since a holy Man was killed in this doleful way, after the Joy as well as the Grace of God had been wonderfully filling of him. This Consideration should keep us from censuring of those that Witchcraft may give disturbance to: But it should put us on studying of our own security. Suppose ye that the Enchanted Family in the Town, were sinners above all the Town, because they have suffered such things? I tell ye nay, but except ye repent, ye may all be so dealt withal. The Father of Lies uttered an awful Truth when he said through the Mouth of a possessed Man, If God would give me leave, I would find enough in the best of you all, to make you all mine.

Consider also, the Misery of them whom Witchcraft may be let loose upon. If David thought it a sad thing to fall into the hands of men, what is it to fall into the hands of Devils? The Hands of Turks, of Spaniards, of Indians, are not so dreadful as those hands that Witches do their works of Darkness by. O what a direful thing is it, to be pricked with Pins, and stabbed with Knives all over, and to be filled all over with broken Bones? 'Tis impossible to reckon up the varieties of miseries which those Monsters inflict where they can have a blow. No less than Death, and that a languishing and a terrible Death will satisfy the Rage of those formidable Dragons. Indeed Witchcraft sometimes grows up into Possession itself: the Devils that are permitted to torment, at last do possess the Bodies of the bewitched sufferers. But who can bear the thoughts of that! who can forbear crying out, O Lord, my flesh trembles for fear of Thee, and I am afraid of Thy Judgments. . . .

Let the Guilty Repent

Let them that have been guilty of Explicit Witchcraft, now also repent of their monstrous and horrid evil in it. If any of you have (I hope none of you have) made an Express Contract with Devils, know that your promise is better broke than kept; it concerns you that you turn immediately from the Power of Satan unto God. Albeit your sin be beyond all expression or conception heinous, yet it is not unpardonable. We read of Manasseh in 2 Chron. 33. 6. He used Enchantments, and used Witchcraft, and dealt with a Familiar

Spirit, and wrought much Evil in the sight of the Lord. But that great Wizzard found Mercy with God, upon his deep Humiliation for it: Such a boundless thing is the Grace of our God! The Prey of Devils, may become the Joy of Angels: The Confederates of Hell, may become the Inhabitants of Heaven, upon their sincere turning unto God. A Witch may be penitent in this, and glorious in another World. There was one Hartford here, who did with much brokenness of Heart own her Witchcraft, and leave her Master, and expire, depending on the Free Grace of God in Christ, and on that word of his, Come to me, ye that labor and are heavy laden, and I will give you rest; and on that, There is a fountain open for sin and for uncleanness. Come then, renounce the Slavery and the Interest of the Devils, renounce your mad League with 'em. Come and give up yourselves unto the Lord Jesus Christ, loathing yourselves exceedingly for your so siding with the black Enemies of his Throne. O come away from the doleful estate you are in. Come away from serving of the Devils that have ensnared your Souls. What Wages have you from those Hellish Taskmasters? Alas you are here among the poor and vile, and ragged Beggars upon Earth. When did Witchcraft ever make any person Rich? And hereafter you must be Objects for the intolerable insolence and cruelty of those Cannibals, and be broken sore in the place of Dragons for evermore. Betake yourselves then to Instant and Constant Prayer, and unto your old filthy Rulers now say, "Depart from me, ye Evil Spirits, for I will keep the Commandments of God."

I Am Not a Witch

Mary Easty and the Salem Court

The Salem witch trials, ignited by the accusations of a group of young girls, remain among the more infamous chapters of colonial American history. Twenty women and men were convicted of witchcraft and executed, 150 more imprisoned. Those initially charged were typical "others" identifiably outside Puritan social norms: Tituba, a slave woman of color from the West Indies, Sarah Osborne, an elderly woman who seldom attended church; Sarah Good, a homeless beggar. But the persecutions soon spread to include ordinary men and women who led generally unremarkable lives.

The charges originated with the bizarre behavior and allegations of Reverend Samuel Parris's daughter Betty, along with her cousin Abigail Williams, friend Mercy Williams, and several other girls. (Tituba and her husband, John Indian, were servants in the Parris household.) Mary Easty, one of the subsequent accused by the girls, was a farmer's wife in her late fifties, mother of seven children. During her first examination, excerpted in the following selection, Easty maintained her innocence despite the accused girls' harrowing demonstrations of "possession" on the floor of the Salem Village meetinghouse that occurred throughout the witch interrogations. Such theatrics proved more persuasive than the defendants' testimony, and Easty was sent off to prison shortly after her examination. But her woes were not over. After two months she was released from incarceration, but the girls seemed to redouble their campaign against her, affecting still more wild fits of "possession" until Easty was rearrested, tried again, and this time, sentenced to death. Her petition, also included here, suggests

Excerpted from *The Salem Witchcraft Papers: Verbatim Transcripts of Legal Documents of the Salem Witchcraft Outbreak of 1692*. Edited by Paul Boyer and Stephen Nissenbaum (Charlottesville: University of Virginia Library: Electronic Text Center, 1938).

Easty's resignation to her fate but also shows her determination to go to the gallows pleading her innocence. In 1711, nearly twenty years after her execution, Easty was vindicated and her surviving family awarded twenty pounds as compensation.

The Salem witch trials continued for months, well into 1693. Their cessation seems to have been due to a decline in public zeal as well as to pressure from Massachusetts governor [William] Phips and conscientious clergymen such as Increase Mather who were increasingly convinced the innocent were being prosecuted and executed. No one convicted of witchcraft has been executed in America since.

As you read, consider the following questions:
1. Compare Easty's attitude in the examination with that suggested in her final petition. How do her tone and language change? Consider specific phrases that suggest a shift in emotion and perspective.
2. Although a good number of accused witches were men, in what ways does the excerpt suggest prevailing Puritan notions about women and their role in society, in the family structure, and as regards children?
3. From the excerpt, what can we surmise about how the Puritans viewed witches? How do the interrogators' questions indicate their expectations about witchcraft?

The Examination of Mary Easty. At a Court held at Salem village Apr. 22 1692 by the Hon. John Hathorne & Jonathan Corwin [magistrates from Salem Township].

[At the bringing in of the accused several [the girls making the allegations] fell into fits.]

Magistrates: Doth this woman hurt you?

[Many mouths were stopped, & several other fits seized them. Abigail Williams said it was Goody [a common title for a housewife] Easty, & she had hurt her, the like said Mary Walcott, & Ann Putman, John Indian said her saw her with Goody Hobbs.]

Magistrates: What do you say, are you guilty?

Easty: I can say before Christ Jesus, I am free.

Magistrates: You see these accuse you.

Easty: There is a God—

Magistrates: Hath she brought the book [of witchcraft, sometimes referred to as a *grimoire*] to you?

[Their mouths were stopped.]

Magistrates: What have you done to these children?

Easty: I know nothing.

Magistrates: How can you say you know nothing, when you see these tormented, & accuse you that you know nothing?

Easty: Would you have me accuse my self?

Magistrates: Yes if you be guilty. How far have you complied with Satan whereby he takes this advantage against you?

Easty: Sir, I never complied but prayed against him all my days, I have no compliance with Satan, in this. What would you have me do?

Magistrates: Confess if you be guilty.

Mary Easty was accused of bewitching the girls and causing them to fall into fits of possession.

Easty: I will say it, if it was my last time, I am clear of this sin.

Magistrates: Of what sin?

Easty: Of witchcraft.

The Accusers Maintain Easty's Guilt

Magistrates: Are you certain this is the woman?

[Never a one could speak for fits. By and by Ann Putman said that was the woman, it was like her, & she told me her name.]

Magistrates: It is marvelous to me that you should sometimes think they are bewitched, & sometimes not, when several confess that they have been guilty of bewitching them.

Easty: Well Sir would you have me confess that that I never knew?

[Her [Easty's] hands were clinched together, & then the hands of Mercy Lewis was clinched.]

Magistrates: Look now your hands are open, her hands are open. Is this the woman?

[They made signs but could not speak, but Ann Putman afterwards Betty Hubbard cried out, "Oh. Goody Easty, Goody Easty you are the woman, you are the woman. Put up her head, for while her head is bowed the necks of these are broken." [The girls are claiming that evil spirits are compelling them to emulate Easty's posture, gestures, etc.]]

Magistrates: What do you say to this?

Easty: Why God will know.

Magistrates: Nay God knows now.

Easty: I know he does.

Magistrates: What did you think of the actions of others before your sisters came out, did you think it was Witchcraft?

Easty: I cannot tell.

Magistrates: Why do you not think it is Witchcraft?

Easty: It is an evil spirit, but whether it be witchcraft I do not know, [Several said she brought them the Book & then they fell into fits.] . . .

The humble petition of Mary [Easty] unto his Excellencies S'r W'm Phips to the honored Judge and Bench now sitting in judicature in Salem and the reverend ministers humbly showeth:

That whereas your poor and humble petition being condemned to die do humbly beg of you to take it into your judicious and pious considerations that your poor and humble petitioner knowing my own innocency. Blessed be the Lord for it and seeing plainly the wiles and subtlety of my accusers by my self can not but judge charitably of others that are going the same way of my self if the Lord steps not mightily in. I was confined a whole month upon the same account that I am condemned now for and then cleared by the afflicted persons as some of your honors know and in two days time I was cried out upon by them and have been confined and now am condemned to die. The Lord above knows my innocency then and likewise does now as at the great day will be known to men and angels—I petition to your honors, not for my own life, for I know I must die and my appointed time is set, but the Lord he knows it is that if it be possible no more innocent blood may be shed which undoubtedly cannot be avoided.

In the way and course you go in I question not but your honors does to the utmost of your powers in the discovery and detecting of witchcraft and witches and would not be guilty of innocent blood for the world but by my own innocency I know you are in the wrong way. The Lord in his infinite mercy direct you in this great work if it be his blessed will that no more innocent blood be shed. I would humbly beg of you that your honors would be pleased to examine these afflicted persons strictly and keep them apart some time and likewise to try some of these confessing witches, I being confident there is several of them has belied themselves and others as will appear if not in this wor[l]d I am sure in the world to come whither I am now a-going and I question not but you'll see an alteration of these things they say [about] my self and others having made a league with the devil we cannot confess I know and the Lord knows as will shortly appear they belie me and so

I question not but they do others. The Lord above who is the searcher of all hearts knows that as I shall answer it at the tribunal seat that I know not the least thing of witchcraft. Therefore I cannot, I dare not, belie my own soul. I beg your honors not to deny this my humble petition from a poor dying innocent person and I question not but the Lord will give a blessing to your endeavors

CHAPTER

4

RELIGIOUS LIFE

CHAPTER PREFACE

Although many of the first English colonists came to America in search of religious freedom, it is important to note that a significant number also strove to impose a strict orthodoxy of their own. Intolerance for doctrinal differences was common, directed not only at such non-Puritan sects as the Quakers but also at dissident Protestants. Back home in England, fierce religious conflicts raged between the royalist Anglican Church of Charles I and Puritan radicals seeking to purge English Protestantism of any remaining vestiges of Roman Catholicism, such as elaborate ceremony, centralized ecclesiastical authority, and other "worldly" trappings. It was not uncommon for the dispute to be imported to the colonies on the eve of the English revolution.

The English civil war broke out in 1639, as the Puritans took up arms to reject the Church of England and the monarchy that supported it. It was a religious war that pitted "Royalist" against "Roundhead" (a common epithet for Puritans referring to their severe haircuts), that saw the execution of King Charles I in 1649 and the ascendancy of Oliver Cromwell, and later the restoration of Charles II to the throne in 1660. But in the New England colonies, the dispute in many places outlasted the war.

Yet the legacy of the Reformation and Martin Luther's original challenge to the worldly authority of what was then the most powerful cultural institution in Europe—the Roman Catholic Church—also influenced more idealistic and tolerant strains of colonial Protestant thought. Like Renaissance humanism, Protestantism put a new value on the individual, asserting the moral preeminence of the conscience. Advocates of religious freedom such as Rhode Island founder Roger Williams invoked biblical principles to support their cause, but their stance had important civil and political ramifications as well, laying the foundation for the notion of separation of church and state ultimately endorsed by the constitutional framers. The Great Awakening, the Calvinist religious revivalism that swelled in early eighteenth-century colonial America, was, despite its emphasis on sin and damnation, a largely democratic movement. Roving preachers delivered theatrical sermons that appealed to a wide congregational audience that traversed class and social boundaries to include the poor, the illiterate, women, and recent, non-English-speaking immigrants. However, true to its Puritan origins, the Great Awakening also encouraged divisiveness and fostered moral superiority among the "saved" over the majority preordained to be eternally damned. Its influence began to wane during the mid-1740s, much to the relief of many more conventional Protestants unnerved by the movement's theatricality and overzealousness.

On Trial for Heresy

Anne Hutchinson and the Puritan General Court

The heresy trial of Anne Hutchinson in 1637 is significant not only for the key doctrinal tenet at stake—justification by faith vs. justification by works—but also for illuminating the role of women in early colonial religious life. Anne Hutchinson, a brilliant, devout woman who had come to the Massachusetts Bay Colony three years before with her husband and family, was active in Puritan intellectual circles that also included theologian John Cotton, minister John Wheelwright (Hutchinson's brother-in-law, referred to as her "brother" in her interrogation), and colonial governor John Winthrop. The Hutchinson home became the site for weekly meetings where women and men gathered to discuss and debate religious matters. Of particular interest to the group was the subject of the Holy Spirit, whose presence in the individual conscience would seem to take precedence over external, human-made laws. Anne Hutchinson's espousal of this strict Calvinist idea that salvation could be achieved by God's grace alone manifest in the Holy Spirit appeared to challenge the authority of the colony's clergy, causing her to be branded an "Antinomian" (one opposed to the law). Moreover, the meetings at her home seemed to threaten the strict gender boundaries dear to most Puritans, as women not only intermingled with men but also spoke out about serious religious issues as though their ideas bore equal merit.

These apparent transgressions resulted in Hutchinson's 1637 trial before the General Court headed by former friend Governor John Winthrop, on charges of heresy. Found guilty, Hutchinson was banished from Massachusetts Bay Colony. But her religious activism did not end,

Excerpted from *History of the Colony and Province of Massachusetts*, by Thomas Hutchinson (Boston, 1767).

and she helped found a Puritan settlement in Portsmouth, Rhode Island. Hutchinson and most of her family were killed by Indians in New York City in 1643.

The following document, which excerpts the trial testimony, makes clear the implications of Hutchinson's alleged offenses. By standing by her beliefs, she is viewed by the court as a threat to the patriarchal hierarchy on a social as well as doctrinal level.

As you read, consider the following questions:
1. What evidence in the transcript do you find that Hutchinson is on trial for bucking male authority as much as church authority?
2. How would you characterize Hutchinson's attitude toward her interrogators? Is she defiant, evasive, argumentative, resigned? Why do you think she behaves the way she does?
3. What about her views makes Hutchinson, in the minds of the General Court, seem so evidently dangerous to the colony and its social order?

———————————————————————————

Mr. Winthrop, governor: Mrs. Hutchinson, you are called here as one of those that have troubled the peace of the commonwealth and the churches here; you are known to be a woman that hath had a great share in the promoting and divulging of those opinions that are causes of this trouble, and . . . you have spoken diverse things as we have been informed very prejudicial to the honor of the churches and ministers thereof, and you have maintained a meeting and an assembly in your house that hath been condemned by the general assembly as a thing not tolerable nor comely in the sight of God nor fitting for your sex, and notwithstanding that was cried down you have continued the same, therefore we have thought good to send for you to understand how things are, that if you be in an erroneous way we may reduce you that so you may become a profitable member here among us, otherwise if you be obstinate in your course that then the court may take such course that you may trouble us no further, therefore I would intreat you to express whether you do not hold and assent in practice to those opinions and factions that have been handled in court already, that is to say, whether you do not justify [Puritan minister and Hutchinson's brother-in-law] Mr. [John] Wheelwright's sermon and the petition.

Mrs. Hutchinson: I am called here to answer before you but I hear no things laid to my charge.

Winthrop: I have told you some already and more I can tell you.

Hutchinson: Name one Sir.

Winthrop: Have I not named some already?

Hutchinson: What have I said or done?

Winthrop: Why for your doings, this you did harbour and countenance those that are parties in this faction that you have heard of.

Hutchinson: That's matter of conscience, Sir.

Winthrop: Your conscience you must keep or it must be kept for you.

Hutchinson: Must not I then entertain the saints because I must keep my conscience.

Winthrop: Say that one brother should commit felony or treason and come to his other brother's house, if he knows him guilty and conceals him he is guilty of the same. It is his conscience to entertain him, but if his conscience comes into act in giving countenance and entertainment to him that hath broken the law he is guilty too. So if you do countenance those that are transgressors of the law you are in the same fact.

Hutchinson: What law do they transgress?

Winthrop: The law of God and of the state.

Hutchinson: In what particular?

Winthrop: Why in this among the rest, whereas the Lord doth say honor thy father and thy mother.

Hutchinson: Aye, Sir in the Lord.

Winthrop: This honor you have broke in giving countenance to them.

Hutchinson: In entertaining those did I entertain them against any act (for there is the thing) or what God hath appointed?

Winthrop: You knew that Mr. Wheelwright did preach this sermon and those that countenance him in this do break a law.

God's Law or Man's Law?

Hutchinson: What law have I broken?

  Winthrop: Why the fifth commandment.

  Hutchinson: I deny that for he saith in the Lord. . . .

  Winthrop: You have counselled them.

  Hutchinson: Wherein?

  Winthrop: Why in entertaining them.

  Hutchinson: What breach of law is that Sir?

  Winthrop: Why, dishonoring of parents.

  Hutchinson: But put the case, Sir, that I do fear the Lord and my parents, may not I entertain them that fear the Lord because my parents will not give me I leave?

Winthrop: If they be the fathers of the commonwealth, and they of another religion, if you entertain them then you dishonor your parents and are justly punishable.

Hutchinson: If I entertain them, as they have dishonored their parents I do.

Winthrop: No but you by countenancing them above others put honor upon them.

Hutchinson: I may put honor upon them as the children of God and as they do honor the Lord.

Winthrop: We do not mean to discourse with those of your sex but only this; you do adhere unto them and do endeavour to set forward this faction and so you do dishonor us.

Hutchinson: I do acknowledge no such thing neither do I think that I ever put any dishonor upon you.

The Nature of Hutchinson's Meetings

Winthrop: Why do you keep such a meeting at your house as you do every week upon a set day?

Hutchinson: It is lawful for me so to do, as it is all your practices and can you find a warrant for yourself and condemn me for the same thing? The ground of my taking it up was, when I first came to this land because I did not go to such meetings as those were, it was presently reported that I did not allow of such meetings but held them unlawful and therefore in that regard they said I was proud and did despise all ordinances, upon that a friend came unto me and told me of it and I to prevent such aspersions took it up, but it was in practice before I came therefore I was not the first.

Winthrop: For this, that you appeal to our practice you need no confutation. If your meeting had answered to the former it had not been offensive, but I will say that there was no meeting of women alone, but your meeting is of another sort for there are sometimes men among you.

Hutchinson: There was never any man with us.

Winthrop: Well, admit there was no man at your meeting and that you was sorry for it, there is no warrant for your doings, and by what warrant do you continue such a course?

Hutchinson: I conceive there lies a clear rule in Titus, that the elder women should instruct the younger [Titus 2:3–5] and then I must have a time wherein I must do it. . . .

Winthrop: But suppose that a hundred men come unto you to be instructed will you forbear to instruct them?

Hutchinson: As far as I conceive I cross a rule in it.

Winthrop: Very well and do you not so here?

Hutchinson: No, Sir, for my ground is they are men.

Winthrop: Men and women all is one for that, but suppose that a man should come and say Mrs. Hutchinson I hear that you are a woman that God hath given his grace unto and you have knowledge in the word of God I pray instruct me a little, ought you not to instruct this man?

Hutchinson: I think I may.—Do you think it not lawful for me to teach women and why do you call me to teach the court?

Winthrop: We do not call you to teach the court but to lay open yourself. . . .

A Matter of Authority

Winthrop: Your course is not to be suffered for, besides that we find such a course as this to be greatly prejudicial to the state, besides the occasion that it is to seduce many honest persons that aye called to those meetings and your opinions being known to be different from the word of God may seduce many simple souls that resort unto you, besides that the occasion which hath come of late hath come from none but such as have frequented your meetings, so that now they are flown off from magistrates and ministers and this since they have come to you, and besides that it will not well stand with the commonwealth that families should be neglected for so many neighbours and dames and so much time spent, we see no rule of God for this, we see not that any should have authority to set up any other exercises besides what authority hath already set up and so what hurt comes of this you will be guilty of and we for suffering you.

Hutchinson: Sir, I do not believe that to be so.

Winthrop: Well, we see how it is we must therefore put it away from you, or restrain you from maintaining this course.

Hutchinson: If you have a rule for it from God's word you may.

Winthrop: We are your judges, and not you ours and we must compel you to it.

Hutchinson: If it please you by authority to put it down I will freely let you for I am subject to your authority. . . .

Women and Men at the Meetings

Mr. [Thomas] Dudley, deputy governor: Here hath been much spoken concerning Mrs. Hutchinson's meetings and among other answers she saith that men come not there, I would ask you this one question then, whether never any man was at your meeting?

Winthrop: There are two meetings kept at their house.

Dudley: How is there two meetings?

Hutchinson: Aye Sir, I shall I not equivocate, there is a meeting of men and women and there is a meeting only for women.

Dudley: Are they both constant?

Hutchinson: No, but upon occasions they are deferred.

Mr. [John] Endicott [churchman on the Council]: Who teaches in the men's meetings none but men, do not women sometimes?

Hutchinson: Never as I heard, not one.

The Charge of Heresy

Dudley: I would go a little higher with Mrs. Hutchinson. About three years ago we were all in peace. Mrs. Hutchinson from that time she came hath made a disturbance, and some that came over with her in the ship did inform me what she was as soon as she was landed. I being then in place dealt with the pastor and teacher of Boston and desired them to enquire of her, and then I was satisfied that she held nothing different from us, but within half a year after, she had vented diverse of her strange opinions and had made parties in the country, and at length it comes that Mr. [John] Cotton and Mr. [Henry] Vane [previous governor of Massachusetts and supporter of Hutchinson] were of her judgment, but Mr. Cotton cleared himself that he was not of that mind, but now it appears by this woman's meeting that Mrs. Hutchinson hath so forestalled the minds of many by their resort to her meeting that now she hath a potent party in the country. Now if all these things have endangered us as from that foundation and if she in particular hath disparaged all our ministers in the land that they have preached a covenant of works, and only Mr. Cotton a covenant of grace, why this is not to be suffered, and therefore being driven to the foundation and it being found that Mrs. Hutchinson is she that hath depraved all the ministers and hath been the cause of what is fallen out, why we must take away the foundation and the building will fall.

Hutchinson: I pray, Sir, prove it that I said they preached nothing but a covenant of works.

Dudley: Nothing but a covenant of works, why a Jesuit may preach truth sometimes.

Hutchinson: Did I ever say they preached a covenant of works then?

Dudley: If they do not preach a covenant of grace clearly, then they preach a covenant of works.

Hutchinson: No Sir, one may preach a covenant of grace more clearly than another, so I said. . . .

Dudley: I will make it plain that you did say that the ministers did preach a covenant of works.

Hutchinson: I deny that. . . .

Dudley: What do I do charging of you if you deny what is so fully proved.

The Witnesses

Winthrop: Here are six undeniable ministers who say it is true and yet you deny that you did say that they did preach a covenant of works and that they were not able ministers of the gospel, and it appears plainly that you have spoken it, and whereas you say that it was drawn from you in a way of friendship, you did profess then that it was out of conscience that you spake and said [that] the fear of man is a snare; wherefore should I be afraid, I will speak plainly and freely.

Hutchinson: That I absolutely deny, for the first question was thus answered by me to them. They thought that I did conceive there was a difference between them and Mr. Cotton. At the first I was somewhat reserved, then said Mr. [Hugh] Peters [minister critical of Hutchinson] I pray answer the question directly as fully and as plainly as you desire we should tell you our minds, Mrs. Hutchinson; we come for plain dealing and telling you our hearts. Then I said I would deal as plainly as I could, and whereas they say I said they were under a covenant of works and in the state of the apostles why these two speeches cross one another. I might say they might preach a covenant of works as did the apostles, but to preach a covenant of works and to be under a covenant of works is another business.

Dudley: There have been six witnesses to prove this and yet you deny it.

Hutchinson: I deny that these were the first words that were spoken.

Winthrop: You make the case worse, for you clearly shew that the ground of your opening your mind was not to satisfy them but to satisfy your own conscience. . . .

Hutchinson: I acknowledge using the words of the apostle to the Corinthians unto him, that they that were ministers of the letter and not the spirit did preach a covenant of works. . . .

Hutchinson Defends Herself

Winthrop: Let us state the case and then we may know what to do. That which is laid to Mrs. Hutchinson's charge is this, that she hath traduced the magistrates and ministers of this jurisdiction, that she hath said the ministers preached a covenant of works and Mr. Cotton a covenant of grace, and that they were not able ministers of the gospel, and she excuses it that she made it a private conference and with a promise of secrecy, &c. now this is charged upon her, and they therefore sent for her seeing she made it her table talk, and then she said the fear of man was a snare and therefore she would not be affeared of them. . . .

Hutchinson: If you please to give me leave I shall give you the ground of what I know to be true. Being much troubled to see the falseness of the constitution of the church of England, I had like to have turned separatist; whereupon I kept a day of solemn humiliation and pondering of the thing; this scripture was brought unto me—he that denies Jesus Christ to be come in the flesh is antichrist—This I considered of and in considering found that the papists did not deny him to be come in the flesh nor we did not deny him—who then was antichrist? . . . The Lord knows that I could not open scripture; he must by his prophetical office open it unto me. . . . I bless the Lord, he hath let me see which was the clear ministry and which the wrong. Since that time I confess I have been more choice and he hath let me to distinguish between the voice of my beloved and the voice of Moses, the voice of John [the]

Baptist and the voice of antichrist, for all those voices are spoken of in scripture. Now if you do condemn me for speaking what in my conscience I know to be truth I must commit myself unto the Lord.

Mr. [Increase] Nowell [Puritan Council member]: How do you know that that was the spirit?

Hutchinson: How did Abraham know that it was God that bid him offer his son, being a breach of the sixth commandment?

Dudley: By an immediate voice.

Hutchinson: So to me by an immediate revelation.

Dudley: How! an immediate revelation.

Hutchinson: By the voice of his own spirit to my soul. I will give you another scripture, Jeremiah 46. 27, 28—out of which the Lord shewed me what he would do for me and the rest of his servants.—But after he was pleased to reveal himself to me. . . . Ever since that time I have been confident of what he hath revealed unto me. . . . Therefore I desire you to look to it, for you see this scripture fulfilled this day and therefore I desire you that as you tender the Lord and the church and commonwealth to consider and look what you do. You have power over my body but the Lord Jesus hath power over my body and soul, and assure yourselves thus much, you do as much as in you lies to put the Lord Jesus Christ from you, and if you go on in this course you begin you wil I bring a curse upon you and your posterity, and the mouth of the Lord hath spoken it. . . .

Verdict and Sentence

Winthrop: The court hath already declared themselves satisfied concerning the things you hear, and concerning the troublesomeness of her spirit and the danger of her course amongst us, which is not to be suffered. Therefore if it be the mind of the court that Mrs. Hutchinson for these things that appear before us is unfit for our society, and if it be the mind of the court that she shall be banished out of our liberties and imprisoned till she be sent away, let them hold up their hands. . . .

Winthrop: Mrs. Hutchinson, the sentence of the court you hear is that you are banished from out of our jurisdiction as being a woman not fit for our society, and are to be imprisoned till the court shall send you away.

Hutchinson: I desire to know wherefore I am banished?

Winthrop: Say no more, the court knows wherefore and is satisfied.

A Plea for Religious Liberty

Roger Williams

If many of the eminent Puritan clergymen of colonial America were known for their fiery Calvinist emphasis on sin and damnation, Roger Williams (1603–1683) stood out as one of the colonies' most ardent early advocates for tolerance and freedom of conscience. Founder of Providence Plantation in 1636 (later to be known as Rhode Island), Williams rejected the polarizing dogmatism that had spawned religious strife and violent revolution in his homeland of England. While many Puritan dissidents had fled to the colonies to escape persecution themselves, they also tended to exhort the same doctrinal orthodoxy that had beleaguered them. Williams, on the other hand, argued passionately for religious pluralism (tolerating even Jewish and Indian beliefs) and the separation of the civil and ecclesiastical realms. Hence Williams was among the first colonial Americans to call for a separation of church and state, a tenet later to become a basic principle for the framers of the Constitution.

In the following excerpt from Williams's 1644 treatise on religious liberty, he challenges the prevailing notion that the Christian state's duty is to impose orthodoxy. Despite the Christian duty to convert the heathen to salvation, Williams maintains that biblical authority forbids the use of secular law to interfere in matters of religious conscience. His argument is structured as a rational disputation—a dialogue between peace and truth—rather than as a fiery diatribe. Radical for the times, Williams's ideas did not sit well with most of his fellow clergy, but resonate today for their revolutionary foresight and embrace of tolerance.

Excerpted from *The Bloudy Tenent of Persecution, for the Cause of Conscience, Discussed in a Conference Between Truth and Peace*, by Roger Williams (Providence, RI: Publications of the Narragansett Club, 1867).

As you read, consider the following questions:
1. How does Williams's argument for religious tolerance lend itself to an endorsement of democracy in general?
2. In what ways does Williams's tract make evident that he is arguing against the dominant views of his fellow Protestants? How does he employ both scriptural and secular history to bolster the religious validity of his position?
3. What is the effect of Williams casting his argument as a dialogue between truth and peace? Is his case for religious tolerance strengthened or weakened by this device, which may seem to grant equal weight to both sides of the dispute?

First, that the blood of so many hundred thousand souls of Protestants and Papists [Catholics], spilt in the wars of present and former ages, for their respective consciences, is not required nor accepted by Jesus Christ the Prince of Peace.

Secondly, pregnant scriptures and arguments are throughout the work proposed against the doctrine of persecution for cause of conscience.

Thirdly, satisfactory answers are given to scriptures, and objections produced by [Protestant theologians] Mr. [John] Calvin, [Theodore] Beza, Mr. [John] Cotton, and the ministers of the New English churches and others former and later, tending to prove the doctrine of persecution for cause of conscience.

Fourthly, the doctrine of persecution for cause of conscience is proved guilty of all the blood of the souls crying for vengeance under the altar.

Fifthly, all civil states with their officers of justice in their respective constitutions and administrations are proved essentially civil, and therefore not judges, governors, or defenders of the spiritual or Christian state and worship.

Sixthly, it is the will and command of God that (since the coming of his Son the Lord Jesus) a permission of the most paganish, Jewish, Turkish, or antichristian consciences and worships, be granted to all men in all nations and countries; and they are only to be fought against with that sword which is only (in soul matters) able to conquer, to wit, the sword of God's Spirit, the Word of God.

Seventhly, the state of the Land of Israel, the kings and people thereof in peace and war, is proved figurative and ceremonial, and no pattern nor president for any kingdom or civil state in the world to follow.

Eighthly, God requireth not a uniformity of religion to be enacted and enforced in any civil state; which enforced uniformity (sooner or later) is the greatest occasion of civil war, ravishing of conscience, persecution of Christ Jesus in his servants, and of the hypocrisy and destruction of millions of souls.

Ninthly, in holding an enforced uniformity of religion in a civil state, we must necessarily disclaim our desires and hopes of the Jew's conversion to Christ.

Tenthly, an enforced uniformity of religion throughout a nation or civil state, confounds the civil and religious, denies the principles of Christianity and civility, and that Jesus Christ is come in the flesh.

Eleventhly, the permission of other consciences and worships than a state professeth only can (according to God) procure a firm and lasting peace (good assurance being taken according to the wisdom of the civil state for uniformity of civil obedience from all forts).

Twelfthly, lastly, true civility and Christianity may both flourish in a state or kingdom, notwithstanding the permission of divers and contrary consciences, either of Jew or Gentile. . . .

Truth and Peace Debate Holy Persecutions

TRUTH. I acknowledge that to molest any person, Jew or Gentile, for either professing doctrine, or practicing worship merely religious or spiritual, it is to persecute him, and such a person (whatever his doctrine or practice be, true or false) suffereth persecution for conscience.

But withal I desire it may be well observed that this distinction is not full and complete: for beside this that a man may be persecuted because he holds or practices what he believes in conscience to be a truth (as Daniel did, for which he was cast into the lions' den, Dan. 6), and many thousands of Christians, because they durst not cease to preach and practice what they believed was by God commanded, as the Apostles answered (Acts 4 & 5), I say besides this a man may also be persecuted, because he dares not be constrained to yield obedience to such doctrines and worships as are by men invented and appointed. . . .

PEACE. Dear TRUTH, I have two sad complaints:

First, the most sober of the witnesses, that dare to plead thy cause, how are they charged to be mine enemies, contentious, turbulent, seditious?

Secondly, shine enemies, though they speak and rail against thee, though they outrageously pursue, imprison, banish, kill thy faithful witnesses, yet how is all vermilion'd o'er for justice against the heretics? Yea, if they kindle coals, and blow the flames of devouring wars, that leave neither spiritual nor civil state, but burn up branch and root, yet how do all pretend an holy war? He that kills, and he that's killed, they both cry out: "It is for God, and for their conscience."

'Tis true, nor one nor other seldom dare to plead the mighty Prince Christ Jesus for their author, yet (both Protestant and Papist) pretend they have spoke with Moses and the Prophets who all, say they (before Christ came), allowed such holy persecutions, holy wars against the enemies of holy church.

TRUTH. Dear PEACE (to ease thy first complaint), 'tis true, thy dearest sons, most like their mother, peacekeeping, peacemaking sons of God, have borne and still must bear the blurs of troublers of Israel, and turners of the world upside down. And 'tis true again, what Solomon once spake: "The beginning of strife is as when one letteth out water, therefore (saith he) leave off contention before it be meddled with. This caveat should keep the banks and sluices firm and strong, that strife, like a breach of waters, break not in upon the sons of men."

Yet strife must be distinguished: It is necessary or unnecessary, godly or ungodly, Christian or unchristian, etc.

It is unnecessary, unlawful, dishonorable, ungodly, unchristian, in most cases in the world, for there is a possibility of keeping sweet peace in most cases, and, if it be possible, it is the express command of God that peace be kept (Rom. 13).

Again, it is necessary, honorable, godly, etc., with civil and earthly weapons to defend the innocent and to rescue the oppressed from the violent paws and jaws of oppressing persecuting Nimrods 2 (Psal. 73; Job 29).

It is as necessary, yea more honorable, godly, and Christian, to fight the fight of faith, with religious and spiritual artillery, and to contend earnestly for the faith of Jesus, once delivered to the saints against all opposers, and the gates of earth and hell, men or devils, yea against Paul himself, or an angel from heaven, if he bring any other faith or doctrine. . . .

Civil Force Is Religion's Enemy

PEACE. I add that a civil sword (as woeful experience in all ages has proved) is so far from bringing or helping forward an opposite in religion to repentance that magistrates sin grievously against the work of God and blood of souls by such proceedings. Because as (commonly) the sufferings of false and antichristian teachers harden their followers, who being blind, by this means are occasioned to tumble into the ditch of hell after their blind leaders, with more inflamed zeal of lying confidence. So, secondly, violence and a sword of steel begets such an impression in the sufferers that certainly they conclude (as indeed that religion cannot be true which needs such instruments of violence to uphold it so) that persecutors are far from soft and gentle commiseration of the blindness of others. . . .

For (to keep to the similitude which the Spirit useth, for instance) to batter down a stronghold, high wall, fort, tower, or castle, men bring not a first and second admonition, and after obstinacy, excommunication, which are spiritual weapons concerning them that be in the church: nor exhortation to repent and be baptized, to believe in the Lord Jesus, etc., which are proper weapons to them that be without, etc. But to take a stronghold, men bring cannons, culverins, saker, bullets, powder, muskets, swords, pikes, etc., and these to this end are weapons effectual and proportionable.

On the other side, to batter down idolatry, false worship, heresy, schism, blindness, hardness, out of the soul and spirit, it is vain, improper, and unsuitable to bring those weapons which are used by persecutors, stocks, whips, prisons, swords, gibbets, stakes, etc. (where these seem to prevail with some cities or kingdoms, a stronger force sets up again, what a weaker pull'd down), but against these spiritual strongholds in the souls of men, spiritual artillery and weapons are proper, which are mighty through God to subdue and bring under the very thought to obedience, or else to bind fast the soul with chains of darkness, and lock it up in the prison of unbelief and hardness to eternity.

Against Toleration

Nathaniel Ward

The Puritans of New England were notoriously intolerant of other religious denominations, despite—or perhaps because of—their own history of persecution in England. They zealously persecuted, banished, and occasionally executed "heretics." Minister Nathaniel Ward, author of the following selection, had himself been excommunicated from the Church of England before settling in Ipswich, Massachusetts. Interestingly, Ward is also considered chief author of the Massachusetts Body of Liberties, influential document advocating many civil liberties that would help lay the foundation of the Bill of Rights. But like many early colonists, Ward was intellectually a man of contradictions. In the following treatise from 1647, Ward sees intolerance as a Christian virtue, and calls on the state as well as the community of believers to enforce his understanding of Puritan orthodoxy.

As you read, consider the following questions:
1. How does Ward define "liberty of conscience"? Compare and contrast his definition with our modern understanding of the term, and/or with Roger Williams's.
2. What are the dangers that Ward associates with religious tolerance? What does he see as the benefits of religious homogeneity, not just for the individual conscience but the community?
3. What is the dominant tone of Ward's treatise? Examine how he uses tone and word choice to emphasize authority to expound on this greatly debated matter.

Excerpted from *The Simple Cobbler of Aggawamm in America,* by Theodore de la Guard (London, 1647).

First, such as have given or taken any unfriendly reports of us New-English, should do well to recollect themselves. We have been reputed a colluvies [medley; slapdash collection] of wild opinionists, swarmed into a remote wilderness to find elbow-room for our fanatic doctrines and practices: I trust our diligence past, and constant sedulity [diligence] against such persons and courses, will plead better things for us. I dare take upon me, to be the herald of New England so far, as to proclaim to the world, in the name of our colony, that all Familists, Antinomians, Anabaptists [ostensibly fanatical radical Protestant sects], and other enthusiasts shall have free liberty to keep away from us, and such as will come to be gone as fast as they can, the sooner the better.

Secondly, I dare aver, that God doth no where in his word tolerate Christian States, to give tolerations to such adversaries of his Truth, if they have power in their hands to suppress them. . . .

Toleration Is Neither a Christian Nor Civic Virture

Not to tolerate things merely indifferent to weak consciences, argues a conscience too strong: pressed uniformity in these, causes much disunity: To tolerate more than indifference, is not to deal indifferently with God: He that doth it, takes his scepter out of his hand, and bids him stand by. Who hath to do to institute religion but God. The power of all religion and ordinances, lies in their purity: their purity in their simplicity: then are mixtures pernicious. I lived in a city, where a Papist [Roman Catholic] preached in one church, a Lutheran in another, a Calvinist in a third—a Lutheran one part of the day, a Calvinist the other, in the same pulpit: the religion of that place was but motley and meager, their affections leopard-like. . . .

That State is wise, that will improve all pains and patience rather to compose, than tolerate differences in Religion. There is no divine truth, but hath much celestial fire in it from the spirit of truth: nor no irreligious untruth, without its proportion of antifire from the spirit of error to contradict it: the zeal of the one, the virulency of the other, must necessarily kindle combustions. Fiery diseases seated in the spirit, embroil the whole frame of the body: others more external and cool, are less dangerous. They which divide in religion, divide in God; they who divide in him, divide beyond Genus Generalissimum [logical term referring to a supreme category], where there is no reconciliation, without atonement—that is, without uniting in him, who is one, and in his truth, which is also one. . . .

And prudent are those Christians, that will rather give what may be given, than hazard all by yielding nothing. To sell all peace of country, to buy some peace of conscience unseasonably, is more avarice than thrift, imprudence than patience: they deal not equally, that set any Truth of God at such a rate; but they deal wisely that will stay till the market is fallen. . . .

More Errors in Toleration
Concerning Tolerations I may further assert.

That persecution of true religion, and toleration of false, are the Jannes and Jambres [traditionally, the names of the magicians in the Egyptian pharaoh's court] to the Kingdom of Christ, whereof the last is far the worst. . . .

He that is willing to tolerate any religion, or discrepant way of religion, besides his own, unless it be in matters merely indifferent, either doubts of his own, or is not sincere in it.

He that is willing to tolerate any unsound opinion, that his own may also be tolerated, though never so sound, will for a need hang God's Bible at the Devil's girdle.

Every toleration of false religions, or opinions hath as many errors and sins in it, as all the false religious and opinions it tolerates, and one sound one more.

On Liberty of Conscience
That State that will give liberty of conscience in matters of religion, must give liberty of conscience and conversation

in their moral laws, or else the fiddle will be out of tune, and some of the strings crack.

He that will rather make an irreligious quarrel with other religions than try the truth of his own by valuable arguments, and peaceable sufferings; either his religion, or himself is irreligious.

Experience will teach churches and Christians, that it is far better to live in a State united, though a little corrupt, than in a State, whereof some part is incorrupt, and all the rest divided.

I am not altogether ignorant of the eight rules given by Orthodox divines about giving tolerations, yet with their favor I dare affirm,

That there is no rule given by God for any State to give an affirmative toleration to any false religion, or opinion whatsoever; they must connive in some cases, but may not concede in any. . . .

That if the State of England shall either willingly tolerate, or weakly connive at such courses, the church of that kingdom will sooner become the Devil's dancing-school,

Puritans worship at a church in Plymouth. The Puritans were known for their intolerance of other religious denominations.

than God's temple: . . . And what pity it is, that that country which hath been the staple of truth to all Christendom, should now become the aviary of errors to the whole world, let every fearing heart judge.

I take liberty of conscience to be nothing but a freedom from sin, and error. . . . And liberty of error nothing but a prison for conscience. Then small will be the kindness of a State to build such prisons for their subjects.

Only One True Religion

The scripture saith, there is nothing makes free but truth, and truth faith, there is no truth but one: If the States of the world would make it their summ-operous care to preserve this one truth in its purity and authority it would case you of all other political cares. I am sure Satan makes it his grand, if not only task, to adulterate truth; falsehood is his sole scepter, whereby he first ruffled, and ever since ruined the world. . . .

There is talk of an universal toleration, I would talk as loud as I could against it, did I know what more apt and reasonable sacrifice England could offer to God for his late performing all his heavenly truths then an universal toleration of all hellish errors, or how they shall make an universal reformation, but by making Christ's academy the Devil's university. . . .

It is said, that men ought to have liberty of their conscience, and that it is persecution to debar them of it: I can rather stand amazed then reply to this: it is an astonishment to think that the brains of men should be parboiled in such impious ignorance; Let all the wits under the heavens lay their heads together and find an assertion worse than this (one excepted) I will petition to be chosen the universal Idiot of the world.

On Tolerating the Quakers

Edward Hart

The first Quakers arrived in the colonies in 1656, and were almost immediately subjected to the same mistreatment they encountered in England. Founded by George Fox in England around 1646, the Quakers shared with the Puritans an emphasis on the individual conscience and rejection of the elaborate ceremonies of the Anglican Church. However, they were branded radicals for their belief in the presence of God's "Light" in all humans, which justified their doctrine of nonviolence and countered the Calvinist doctrine of the elect, which held that humans were divided into distinct groups of "saved" and "damned."

With the exception of Rhode Island (which had become a haven for religious dissidents), the colonies of New England zealously persecuted the Quakers. Puritans in Massachusetts were especially intolerant; Quakers were routinely stripped naked and whipped through the streets, branded with hot irons, mutilated by having their ears cut off, and in extreme cases, executed. Ironically, it was the restoration of the English monarchy that prompted a 1661 edict from Charles II ordering the colonies to cease persecuting Quakers. The king would bestow upon William Penn a colonial land grant in 1681, which would establish the first Quaker settlement in America. But even before the Restoration, the citizens of Flushing, New York, issued in 1657 their "remonstrance" to New Amsterdam governor Peter Stuyvesant, who had endorsed the persecution of Quakers. In the document, drafted by a minister named Edward Hart, the citizens urged tolerance for all religions, not just for the Quakers and other

Excerpted from *Remonstrance of the Inhabitants of the Town of Flushing to Governor Stuyvesant*, by Edward Hart (New York: New York Historical Records, 1657).

Christian sects but also for Jews, Muslims, and unspecified "Independents." The Flushing Remonstrance marks the first time in America that a community went on record to demand religious liberty from its government.

As you read, consider the following questions:
1. How do the petitioners make use of both civil and biblical authority to support their argument in favor of religious tolerance?
2. What are the values that the citizens seem to want their colony to embody? What may we infer they see as the duty of government to the people?
3. Like Roger Williams, the Flushing colonists seek a wide-ranging religious tolerance. Compare their arguments and note the different strategies the two texts employ to support the same basic assertion. Consider too the role readership plays in the ways the texts approach the topic.

To Governor Stuyvesant December 27, 1657
Right Honorable,
You have been pleased to send up unto us a certain prohibition or command that we should not receive or entertain any of those people called Quakers because they are supposed to be by some, seducers of the people. For our part we cannot condemn them in this case, neither can we stretch out our hands against them, to punish, banish or persecute them for out of Christ God is a consuming fire, and it is a fearful thing to fall into the hands of the living God.

We desire therefore in this case not to judge least we be judged, neither to condemn least we be condemned, but rather let every man stand and fall to his own Master. We are bound by the law to do good unto all men, especially to those of the household of faith. And though for the present we seem to be unsensible of the law and the law giver, yet when death and the law assault us, if we have our advocate to seek, who shall plead for us in this case of conscience betwixt God and our own souls; the powers of this world can neither attack us, neither excuse us, for if God justify who can condemn and if God condemn there is none can justify.

Scriptural and Civil Law

And for those jealousies and suspicions which some have of them, that they are destructive unto magistracy and minssereye [ministry], that can not be, for the magistrate hath the sword in his hand and the minister hath the sword in his hand, as witness those two great examples which all magistrates and ministers are to follow, Moses and Christ, whom God raised up maintained and defended against all the enemies both of flesh and spirit; and therefore that which is of God will stand, and that which is of man will come to nothing. And as the Lord hath taught Moses or the civil power to give an outward liberty in the state by the law written in his heart designed for the good of all, and can truly judge who is good, who is civil, who is true and who is false, and can pass definite sentence of life or death against that man which rises up against the fundamental law of the States General; so he hath made his ministers a savor of life unto life, and a savor of death unto death.

The law of love, peace and liberty in the states extending to Jews, Turks, and Egyptians, as they are considered the sons of Adam, which is the glory of the outward state of Holland, so love, peace and liberty, extending to all in Christ Jesus, condemns hatred, war and bondage. And because our Savior saith it is impossible but that offenses will come, but woe unto him by whom they cometh, our desire is not to offend one of his little ones, in whatsoever form, name or title he appears in, whether Presbyterian, Independent, Baptist or Quaker, but shall be glad to see anything of God in any of them, desiring to doe unto all men as we desire all men should do unto us, which is the true law both of Church and State; for our Savior saith this is the law and the prophets.

All Religions Will Be Tolerated

Therefore, if any of these said persons come in love unto us, we cannot in conscience lay violent hands upon them, but give them free egress and regress unto our town, and houses, as God shall persuade our consciences. And in this we are true subjects both of Church and State, for we are bound by the law of God and man to do good unto all men and evil to no man. And this is according to the patent and charter of our Town, given unto us in the name of the States General, which we are not willing to infringe, and violate, but shall hold to our patent and shall remain, your humble subjects, the inhabitants of [Flushing].

Sinners in the Hands of an Angry God

Jonathan Edwards

Characterizations of the Puritans of New England range from the relatively secular and benign Plymouth pilgrims to the fanatical witch-hunters of Salem. The Puritans were not an explicitly defined sect or denomination, as were the Quakers or Anglicans. Puritanism then as now was a somewhat fluid term that could encompass a variety of religious beliefs, but from a theological standpoint, "true" Puritans were Protestants whose views were shaped predominantly by the tenets put forth by Swiss theologian John Calvin. Like fellow sixteenth-century reformer Martin Luther, Calvin rejected the authority of the papacy and the notion of free will. He espoused the doctrines of predestination and election, which held that God chose those few souls (the "elect") He would save before their birth, irrespective of human agency. Unless an individual experienced God's grace in his or her conscience, that person was damned to hellfire. Earthly misfortunes were likewise seen as the tangible evidence of God's damning wrath, whether on an individual, a family, or a community.

Colonial Puritanism found formidable and mighty proponents in such clergymen as Cotton Mather, Increase Mather (father of Cotton), and others, but perhaps none more eloquent in the severity of his Calvinist invective as Jonathan Edwards (1703–1758). Connecticut-born and Yale-educated, Edwards served for over twenty years as minister of the Congregational Church in Northampton, Massachusetts, and is credited for the colonial religious revival known as "the Great Awakening." His Puritan extremism caused his dis-

Excerpted from "Sinners in the Hands of an Angry God," by Jonathan Edwards, *The Works of Jonathan Edwards*, edited by Edward Hickman (Northampton, MA, 1834).

missal from his Northampton post in 1750. Undaunted, Edwards turned to missionary work among the Indians of Stockbridge. He died in 1757 after a smallpox inoculation, ironically a medical innovation avidly promoted by his great Calvinist forerunner Cotton Mather.

In the following excerpt from Edwards's most famous sermon, "Sinners in the Hands of an Angry God" (1741), he touches forcefully on his favorite themes of human wickedness and helplessness against God's just vengeance. While Edwards seems to offer a faint glimmer of salvation to the few congregants capable of realizing the depths of their depravity and repenting, his emphasis is clearly on the horrors of damnation and the fierce inexorability of God's will.

As you read, consider the following questions:
1. Regardless of its rather ominous content, what qualities make Edwards's sermon interesting as a public address? Consider his use of scriptural citations, his word choice, and the structure of the sermon.
2. Edwards often uses God's hand as a metaphor. List some of the abilities (or uses) of God's hand in the sermon.
3. Can you think of any ways in which such sermons as this might have been seen as not merely frightening or humbling, but as potentially dangerous to the community and social stability?

Their foot shall slide in due time (Deut. 32:35).

In this verse is threatened the vengeance of God on the wicked unbelieving Israelites, who were God's visible people, and who lived under the means of grace; but who, notwithstanding all God's wonderful works towards them, remained (as ver. 28.) void of counsel, having no understanding in them. Under all the cultivations of heaven, they brought forth bitter and poisonous fruit; as in the two verses next preceding the text. The expression I have chosen for my text, Their foot shall slide in due time, seems to imply the following doings, relating to the punishment and destruction to which these wicked Israelites were exposed.

1. That they were always exposed to destruction; as one that stands or walks in slippery places is always exposed to fall. This is implied in the manner of their destruction coming upon them, being represented by their foot sliding. The same is expressed [in] Psalm 73:18. "Surely thou didst set them in slippery places; thou castedst them down into destruction."

2. It implies, that they were always exposed to sudden unexpected destruction. As he that walks in slippery places is every moment liable to fall, he cannot foresee one moment whether he shall stand or fall the next; and when he does fall, he falls at once without warning: Which is also expressed in Psalm 73:18, 19: "Surely thou didst set them in slippery places; thou castedst them down into destruction: How are they brought into desolation as in a moment!"

3. Another thing implied is, that they are liable to fall of themselves, without being thrown down by the hand of another; as he that stands or walks on slippery ground needs nothing but his own weight to throw him down.

4. That the reason why they are not fallen already, and do not fall now, is only that God's appointed time is not come. For it is said, that when that due time, or appointed time comes, their foot shall slide. Then they shall be left to fall, as they are inclined by their own weight. God will not hold them up in these slippery places any longer, but will let them go; and then at that very instant, they shall fall into destruction; as he that stands on such slippery declining ground, on the edge of a pit, he cannot stand alone, when he is let go he immediately falls and is lost.

The observation from the words that I would now insist upon is this. "There is nothing that keeps wicked men at any one moment out of hell, but the mere pleasure of God." By the mere pleasure of God, I mean his sovereign pleasure, his arbitrary will, restrained by no obligation, hindered by no manner of difficulty, any more than if nothing else but God's mere will had in the least degree, or in any respect whatsoever, any hand in the preservation of wicked men one moment. The truth of this observation may appear by the following considerations.

The Wrath of God Is Just

1. There is no want of power in God to cast wicked men into hell at any moment. Men's hands cannot be strong when God rises up. The strongest have no power to resist him, nor can any deliver out of his hands. He is not only able to cast wicked men into hell, but he can most easily do it. Sometimes an earthly prince meets with a great deal of difficulty to subdue a rebel, who has found means to fortify himself, and has made himself strong by the numbers of his followers. But it is not so with God. There is no fortress that is any defense from the power of God. Though hand join in hand, and vast multitudes of God's enemies combine and associate themselves, they are easily broken in pieces. They are as great heaps of light chaff before the whirlwind; or large quantities of dry stubble before devouring flames. We find it easy to tread on and crush a worm that we see crawling on the earth; so it is easy for us to cut or singe a slender thread that any thing hangs by: thus easy is it for God, when he pleases, to cast his enemies down to hell. What are we, that we should think to stand before him, at whose rebuke the earth trembles, and before whom the rocks are thrown down?

2. They deserve to be cast into hell; so that divine justice never stands in the way, it makes no objection against God's using his power at any moment to destroy them. Yea, on the contrary, justice calls aloud for an infinite punishment of their sins. Divine justice says of the tree that brings forth such grapes of Sodom, "Cut it down, why cumbereth it the ground?" (Luke xiii. 7). The sword of divine justice is every moment brandished over their heads, and it is nothing but the hand of arbitrary mercy, and God's mere will, that holds it back.

3. They are already under a sentence of condemnation to hell. They do not only justly deserve to be cast down thither, but the sentence of the law of God, that eternal and

immutable rule of righteousness that God has fixed between him and mankind, is gone out against them, and stands against them; so that they are bound over already to hell. John iii. 18. "He that believeth not is condemned already." So that every unconverted man properly belongs to hell; that is his place; from thence he is, (John viii. 23): "Ye are from beneath." And thither be is bound; it is the place that justice, and God's word, and the sentence of his unchangeable law assign to him.

4. They are now the objects of that very same anger and wrath of God, that is expressed in the torments of hell. And the reason why they do not go down to hell at each moment, is not because God, in whose power they are, is not then very angry with them; as he is with many miserable creatures now tormented in hell, who there feel and bear the fierceness of his wrath. Yea, God is a great deal more angry with great numbers that are now on earth: yea, doubtless, with many that are now in this congregation, who it may be are at ease, than he is with many of those who are now in the flames of hell.

So that it is not because God is unmindful of their wickedness, and does not resent it, that he does not let loose his hand and cut them off. God is not altogether such an one as themselves, though they may imagine him to be so. The wrath of God burns against them, their damnation does not slumber; the pit is prepared, the fire is made ready, the furnace is now hot, ready to receive them; the flames do now rage and glow. The glittering sword is whet, and held over them, and the pit hath opened its mouth under them.

Wickedness and the Devil
5. The devil stands ready to fall upon them, and seize them as his own, at what moment God shall permit him. They belong to him; he has their souls in his possession, and under his dominion. The scripture represents them as his goods (Luke 11:12). The devils watch them; they are ever by them at their right hand; they stand waiting for them, like greedy hungry lions that see their prey, and expect to

have it, but are for the present kept back. If God should withdraw his hand, by which they are restrained, they would in one moment fly upon their poor souls. The old serpent is gaping for them; hell opens its mouth wide to receive them; and if God should permit it, they would be hastily swallowed up and lost.

6. There are in the souls of wicked men those hellish principles reigning, that would presently kindle and flame out into hell fire, if it were not for God's restraints. There is laid in the very nature of carnal men, a foundation for the torments of hell. There are those corrupt principles, in reigning power in them, and in full possession of them, that are seeds of hell fire. These principles are active and powerful, exceeding violent in their nature, and if it were not for the restraining hand of God upon them, they would soon break out, they would flame out after the same manner as the same corruptions, the same enmity does in the hearts of damned souls, and would beget the same torments as they do in them. The souls of the wicked are in scripture compared to the troubled sea (Isa. 57:20). For the present, God restrains their wickedness by his mighty power, as he does the raging waves of the troubled sea, saying, "Hitherto shalt thou come, but no further;" but if God should withdraw that restraining power, it would soon carry all before it. Sin is the ruin and misery of the soul; it is destructive in its nature; and if God should leave it without restraint, there would need nothing else to make the soul perfectly miserable. The corruption of the heart of man is immoderate and boundless in its fury; and while wicked men live here, it is like fire pent up by God's restraints, whereas if it were let loose, it would set on fire the course of nature; and as the heart is now a sink of sin, so if sin was not restrained, it would immediately turn the soul into a fiery oven, or a furnace of fire and brimstone.

7. It is no security to wicked men for one moment, that there are no visible means of death at hand. It is no security to a natural man, that he is now in health, and that he does not see which way he should now immediately go out of the world by any accident, and that there is no visible danger in

any respect in his circumstances. The manifold and continual experience of the world in all ages, shows this is no evidence, that a man is not on the very brink of eternity, and that the next step will not be into another world. The unseen, unthought-of ways and means of persons going suddenly out of the world are innumerable and inconceivable. Unconverted men walk over the pit of hell on a rotten covering, and there are innumerable places in this covering so weak that they will not bear their weight, and these places are not seen. The arrows of death fly unseen at noon-day; the sharpest sight cannot discern them. God has so many different unsearchable ways of taking wicked men out of the world and sending them to hell, that there is nothing to make it appear, that God had need to be at the expense of a miracle, or go out of the ordinary course of his providence, to destroy any wicked man, at any moment. All the means that there are of sinners going out of the world, are so in God's hands, and so universally and absolutely subject to his power and determination, that it does not depend at all the less on the mere will of God, whether sinners shall at any moment go to hell, than if means were never made use of, or at all concerned in the case.

Human Helplessness
8. Natural men's prudence and care to preserve their own lives, or the care of others to preserve them, do not secure them a moment. To this, divine providence and universal experience do also bear testimony. There is this clear evidence that men's own wisdom is no security to them from death; that if it were otherwise we should see some difference between the wise and politic men of the world, and others, with regard to their liableness to early and unexpected death: but how is it in fact? (Eccles. ii. 16) "How dieth the wise man? even as the fool."

9. All wicked men's pains and contrivance which they use to escape hell, while they continue to reject Christ, and so remain wicked men, do not secure them from hell one moment. Almost every natural man that hears of hell, flatters

himself that he shall escape it; he depends upon himself for his own security; he flatters himself in what he has done, in what he is now doing, or what he intends to do. Every one lays out matters in his own mind how he shall avoid damnation, and flatters himself that he contrives well for himself, and that his schemes will not fail. They hear indeed that there are but few saved, and that the greater part of men that have died heretofore are gone to hell; but each one imagines that he lays out matters better for his own escape than others have done. He does not intend to come to that place of torment; he says within himself, that he intends to take effectual care, and to order matters so for himself as not to fail.

But the foolish children of men miserably delude themselves in their own schemes, and in confidence in their own strength and wisdom; they trust to nothing but a shadow. The greater part of those who heretofore have lived under the same means of grace, and are now dead, are undoubtedly gone to hell; and it was not because they were not as wise as those who are now alive: it was not because they did not lay out matters as well for themselves to secure their own escape. If we could speak with them, and inquire of them, one by one, whether they expected, when alive, and when they used to hear about hell ever to be the subjects of that misery: we doubtless, should hear one and another reply, "No, I never intended to come here: I had laid out matters otherwise in my mind; I thought I should contrive well for myself: I thought my scheme good. I intended to take effectual care; but it came upon me unexpected; I did not look for it at that time, and in that manner; it came as a thief: Death outwitted me: God's wrath was too quick for me. Oh, my cursed foolishness! I was flattering myself, and pleasing myself with vain dreams of what I would do hereafter; and when I was saying, Peace and safety, then suddenly destruction came upon me.

God Owes No Redemption

10. God has laid himself under no obligation, by any promise to keep any natural man out of hell one moment.

God certainly has made no promises either of eternal life, or of any deliverance or preservation from eternal death, but what are contained in the covenant of grace, the promises that are given in Christ, in whom all the promises are yea and amen. But surely they have no interest in the promises of the covenant of grace who are not the children of the covenant, who do not believe in any of the promises, and have no interest in the Mediator of the covenant.

So that, whatever some have imagined and pretended about promises made to natural men's earnest seeking and knocking, it is plain and manifest, that whatever pains a natural man takes in religion, whatever prayers he makes, till he believes in Christ, God is under no manner of obligation to keep him a moment from eternal destruction.

So that, thus it is that natural men are held in the hand of God, over the pit of hell; they have deserved the fiery pit, and are already sentenced to it; and God is dreadfully provoked, his anger is as great towards them as to those that are actually suffering the executions of the fierceness of his wrath in hell, and they have done nothing in the least to appease or abate that anger, neither is God in the least bound by any promise to hold them up one moment; the devil is waiting for them, hell is gaping for them, the flames gather and flash about them, and would fain lay hold on them, and swallow them up; the fire pent up in their own hearts is struggling to break out: and they have no interest in any Mediator, there are no means within reach that can be any security to them. In short, they have no refuge, nothing to take hold of, all that preserves them every moment is the mere arbitrary will, and uncovenanted, unobliged forbearance of an incensed God.

The Purpose of the Sermon

The use of this awful subject may be for awakening unconverted persons in this congregation. This that you have heard is the case of every one of you that are out of Christ. That world of misery, that lake of burning brimstone, is extended abroad under you. There is the dreadful pit of the glowing flames of the wrath of God; there is hell's wide gaping mouth open; and you have nothing to stand upon, nor any thing to take hold of, there is nothing between you and hell but the air; it is only the power and mere pleasure of God that holds you up.

You probably are not sensible of this; you find you are kept out of hell, but do not see the hand of God in it; but look at other things, as the good state of your bodily constitution, your care of your own life, and the means you use for your own preservation. But indeed these things are nothing; if God should withdraw his hand, they would avail no more to keep you from falling, than the thin air to hold up a person that is suspended in it.

Your wickedness makes you as it were heavy as lead, and to tend downwards with great weight and pressure towards hell; and if God should let you go, you would immediately sink and swiftly descend and plunge into the bottomless gulf, and your healthy constitution, and your own care and prudence, and best contrivance, and all your righteousness, would have no more influence to uphold you and keep you out of hell, than a spider's web would have to stop a falling rock. Were it not for the sovereign pleasure of God, the earth would not bear you one moment; for you are a burden to it; the creation groans with you; the creature is made subject to the bondage of your corruption, not willingly; the sun does not willingly shine upon you to give you light to serve sin and Satan; the earth does not willingly yield her increase to satisfy your lusts; nor is it willingly a stage for your wickedness to be acted upon; the air does not willingly serve you for breath to maintain the flame of life in your vitals, while you spend your life in the service of God's enemies. God's creatures are good, and were made for men to serve God with, and do not willingly subserve to any other purpose, and groan when they are abused to purposes so directly contrary to their nature and end. And the world would spew you out, were it not for the sovereign hand of him who hath subjected it in hope. There are black clouds of God's wrath now hanging directly over your heads, full of the dreadful storm, and big with thunder; and were it not for the re- straining hand of God, it would immediately burst forth upon you. The sovereign pleasure of God, for the present, stays his rough wind; otherwise it would come with fury, and your destruction would come like a whirlwind, and you would be like the chaff of the summer threshing floor.

The wrath of God is like great waters that are dammed for the present; they increase more and more, and rise higher and higher, till an outlet is given; and the longer the stream is stopped, the more rapid and mighty is its course, when once it is let loose. It is true, that judgment against your evil works has not been executed hitherto; the floods of God's vengeance have been withheld; but your guilt in the mean time is constantly increasing, and you are every day treasuring up more wrath; the waters are constantly rising, and waxing more and more mighty; and there is nothing but the mere pleasure of God, that holds the wa- ters back, that are unwilling to be stopped, and press hard to go forward. If God should only withdraw his hand from the flood-gate, it would immediately fly open, and the fiery floods of the fierceness and wrath of God, would rush forth with inconceivable fury, and would come upon you with omnipotent power; and if your strength were ten thousand times greater than it is, yea, ten thousand times greater than the strength of the stoutest, sturdiest devil in hell, it would be nothing to withstand or endure it.

Repent and Reform

The bow of God's wrath is bent, and the arrow made ready on the string, and justice bends the arrow at your heart, and strains the bow, and it is nothing but the mere pleasure of God, and that of an angry God, without any promise or obligation at all, that keeps the arrow one moment from being made drunk with your blood. Thus all you that never passed under a great change of heart, by the mighty power of the Spirit of God upon your souls; all you that were never born again, and made new creatures, and raised from being dead in sin, to a state of new, and before altogether unexperienced light and life, are in the hands of an angry God. However you may have reformed your life in many things, and may have had religious affections, and may keep up a form of religion in your families and closets, and in the house of God, it is nothing but his mere pleasure that keeps you from being this moment swallowed up in everlasting destruction. However unconvinced you may now be of the truth of what you hear, by and by you will be fully convinced of it. Those that are gone from being in the like circumstances with you, see that it was so with them; for destruction came suddenly upon most of them; when they expected nothing of it, and while they were saying, Peace and safety: now they see, that those things on which they depended for peace and safety, were nothing but thin air and empty shadows.

The God that holds you over the pit of hell, much as one holds a spider, or some loathsome insect over the fire, abhors you, and is dreadfully provoked: his wrath towards you burns like fire; he looks upon you as worthy of nothing else, but to be cast into the fire; he is of purer eyes than to bear to have you in his sight; you are ten thousand times more abominable in his eyes, than the most hateful venomous serpent is in ours. You have offended him infinitely more than ever a stubborn rebel did his prince; and yet it is nothing but his hand that holds you from falling into the fire every moment. It is to be ascribed to nothing else, that you did not go to hell the last night; that you was suffered to awake again in this world, after you closed your eyes to sleep. And there is no other reason to be given, why you have not dropped into hell since you arose in the morning, but that God's hand has held you up. There is no other reason to be given why you have not gone to hell, since you have sat here in the house of God, provoking his pure eyes by your sinful wicked manner of attending his solemn worship. Yea, there is nothing else that is to be given as a reason why you do not this very moment drop down into hell.

O sinner! Consider the fearful danger you are in: it is a

great furnace of wrath, a wide and bottomless pit, full of the fire of wrath, that you are held over in the hand of that God, whose wrath is provoked and incensed as much against you, as against many of the damned in hell. You hang by a slender thread, with the flames of divine wrath flashing about it, and ready every moment to singe it, and burn it asunder; and you have no interest in any Mediator, and nothing to lay hold of to save yourself, nothing to keep off the flames of wrath, nothing of your own, nothing that you ever have done, nothing that you can do, to induce God to spare you one moment.

5

LAWS AND RULES OF CONDUCT

CHAPTER PREFACE

The geographical distance between England and the New World necessitated a relative autonomy from the very beginning that would, of course, ultimately fuel the colonists' cry for independence. But the first colonies in Virginia and New England did not explicitly conceive of their respective societies, laws, and mode of governance as radical revisions of their British forebears. Only "extremists" like Roger Williams, the founder of the Rhode Island colony, advocated the then-revolutionary notion of separation of church and state. For the most part, the English settlers opposed religious pluralism and accepted the conventional position that the rules of God and those of humans were inherently intertwined. Recusancy laws, mandating regular church attendance, became the norm in colonial legal codes just as they were in England. Lewd, idle, and drunken behavior were not seen as private matters but were subject to fines, public castigation, and, in the most extreme cases, torture, imprisonment, and death. Yet in other important ways colonial legislation did reflect key differences, if often only nuanced ones, from the English model. Theoretically, colonial laws and governance were derived from English Common Law and the Bible. In practice, the very motives that spurred the settlers across the ocean influenced the administration and regulation of their societies.

The notion of representative self-government, even before philosophers John Locke and Thomas Hobbes debated the philosophical concept of the so-called social contract, underlies the early seventeenth-century legal codes of the first colonists. For many of the settlers, self-government was deeply bound up in their reasons for leaving England in the first place. The Puritans generally mistrusted the arbitrary authority they observed wielded by James I and, more emphatically, by his heir, Charles I, especially after the latter abolished Parliament and endorsed Archbishop William Laud's efforts to more closely align the Anglican Church with the practices of the Roman Catholic Church. As for the Virginia colonists (most of whom were Royalists), many were induced to settle in the New World by promises of land and some mode of self-government; this linkage of property rights and self-government would, of course, prove pivotal for the constitutional framers. Similarly, the early calls for a colonial union were informed by not only common security interests but also by a belief that the law should not be arbitrary, designating a given act a crime in one colony but not in others. The early colonists conceived of their societies in pragmatic as much as ideological terms, yet the seeds of a radically new form of governance as well as the values of a rigid, repressive culture may be identified in the legal codes of the day.

Puritan Influence on Virginia Law

Virginia General Assembly

Readers and historians alike have frequently focused on the differences rather than likenesses between the first colonies in Virginia and New England. Certainly the settlers came to the New World with different motives and goals. The Jamestown colonists were prospective entrepreneurs in pursuit of personal fortunes (mainly through tobacco) as well as rewards from the Crown for cementing England's foothold in North America. The Puritans of New England were seeking both religious freedom and (perhaps paradoxically) religious homogeneity. Yet contrasts suggest a false opposition between the two groups of settlers. The following selection demonstrates that the Virginia colonists viewed legal, moral, and religious obligations as no less interlocking than did their Puritan brethren.

A 1618 charter invested the colonial governor, a six-man council, and a representative assembly comprised of twenty burgesses with legal authority theretofore located across the Atlantic in England. The first assembly took place on July 30, 1619, and lasted for six days. Out of this meeting came a host of laws and regulations addressing matters ranging from dealings with the Indians to the enforcement of moral, pious behavior among the colonists. Note that the Church is characterized as a copartner with civil authority in identifying crime and administering punishment. And while sumptuary laws (i.e., the prohibition of "excessive" or otherwise inappropriate apparel) is often associated with Puritan austerity, the Virginia General Assembly's iteration of such laws is a reminder that the concern over social and

Excerpted from *Laws of the Virginia General Assembly*, 1619.

moral propriety was equally as entrenched in more-or-less secular culture as in explicitly sectarian realms.

As you read, consider the following questions:
1. Consider the Church's public function in enforcing laws and prescribing punishment. Can you think of any practical reasons as well as moral ones for the clergy's involvement in law and order in colonial Jamestown?
2. Even though the Virginia General Assembly enacted laws similar to those of the Puritan colonies, what, if any, differences do you notice in the tone and language of the documents?
3. Why do you think excessive apparel was held to be a vice along with drunkenness, idleness, and sexual misconduct? What "sins" seem to be associated with flamboyant or inappropriate dress?

All ministers in the colony shall once a year, namely, in the month of March, bring to the Secretary of Estate a true account of all Christenings, burials and marriages, upon pain, if they fail, to be censured for their negligence by the Governor and Counsel of Estate; likewise, where there be no ministers, that the commanders of the place do supply the same duty.

All ministers shall duly read divine service, and exercise their ministerial function according to the ecclesiastical laws and orders of the Church of England, and every Sunday in the afternoon shall catechize such as are not yet ripe to come to the [church services]. And whosoever of them shall be found negligent or faulty in this kind shall be subject to the censure of the governor and Counsel of Estate.

The ministers and churchwardens shall seek to present all ungodly disorders, the committers whereof if, upon good admonitions and mild reproof, they will not forbear the said scandalous offenses, as suspicions of whoredoms, dishonest company keeping with women and such like, they are to be presented and punished accordingly.

If any person after two warnings, does not amend his or her life in point of evident suspicion of incontinency or of the commission of any other enormous sins, that then he or she be presented by the churchwardens and suspended for a time from the church by the minister. In which Interim if the same person do not amend and humbly submit him or herself to the church, he is then fully to be excommunicated and soon after a writ or warrant to be sent from the governor for the apprehending of his person and seizing on all his goods.

Provided always, that all the ministers do meet once a quarter, namely, at the feast of St. Michael the Archangel, of the nativity of our saviour, of the Annunciation of the blessed Virgin, and about midsummer, at James city [Jamestown] or any other place where the governor shall reside, to determine whom it is fit to excommunicate, and that they first present their opinion to the governor ere they proceed to the act of excommunication.

For the reformation of swearing, every freeman and Mr. [master] of a family after thrice admonition shall give 5s [shillings] or the value upon present demand, to the use of the church where he dwelleth; and every servant after the like admonition, except his Mr. discharge the fine, shall be subject to whipping. Provided, that the payment of the fine notwithstanding, the said servant shall acknowledge his fault publicly in the church.

All persons whatsoever upon the Sabbath day shall frequent divine service and sermons both forenoon and afternoon, and all such as bear arms shall bring their pieces swords, poulder and shot. And every one that shall transgress this law shall forfeit three shillings a time to the use of the church, all lawful and necessary impediments excepted. But if a servant in this case shall willfully neglect his Mr.'s command he shall suffer bodily punishment.

Against Idleness, Gambling, Drunkenness, and Excess

Against idleness, gaming, drunkenness and excess in apparel the Assembly hath enacted as followeth:

First, in detestation of idleness be it enacted, that if any man be fond to live as an Idler or renagade, though a freedman, it shall be lawful for that incorporation or plantation to which he belongeth to appoint him a Mr. to serve for wages, till he show apparent signs of amendment.

Against gaming at dice and cards be it ordained by this present assembly that the winner or winners shall lose all his or their winnings and both winners and losers shall forfeit ten shillings a man, one ten shillings whereof to go to the discoverer, and the rest to charitable and pious uses in the incorporation where the fault is committed.

Against drunkenness be it also decreed that if any private person be found culpable thereof, for the first time he is to be reproved privately by the minister, the second time publicly, the third time to lie in bolts 12 hours in the house of the provost marshall and to pay his fee, and if he still continue in that vice, to undergo such severe punishment as the governor and Counsel of Estate shall think fit to be inflicted on him. But if any officer offend in this crime, the first time he shall receive reproof from the governor, the second time he shall openly be reproved in the church by the minister, and the third time he shall first be committed and then degraded. Provided it be understood that the governor hath always power to restore him when he shall in his discretion think fit.

Against excess in apparel that every man be cessed in the church for all public contributions, if he be unmarried according to his owne apparel, if he be married, according to his own and his wives, or either of their apparel.

Stricter Laws Will Restore God's Favor

The Massachusetts General Court

Because the Puritans generally denied the existence of free human will, they tended to identify the hand of God in both worldly fortunes and worldly woes. Just as Plymouth governor William Bradford saw the decimation of the Indian population by disease as a token of God's favor toward the fledgling colony, some fifty years later the Puritans of Massachusetts viewed the outbreak of King Philip's War (1675–1676) as a sign of God's wrath.

The following document, produced by the Massachusetts General Court in November 1675, addresses the ostensibly rampant immorality that had subjected the colony to divine retribution via the Wampanoag war. It is significant that the laws issue no explicit directives regarding the Indians; the conflict with Metacomet and his people had eroded any distinction between Native Americans who had converted to Christianity and those still "barbarous heathens." But the General Court found no shortage of scapegoats for the current crisis: Quakers, idlers, fops (i.e., the flamboyantly apparelled), and unruly young people all fall under the court's scrutiny and approbation.

As you read, consider the following questions:
1. Notice the prefatory reference to the Indian war, and the absence thereafter of any further allusions to the conflict. What assumptions does the Court seem to be making about the relation of each specific vice they proscribe with the present troubles?

Excerpted from *Records of the Governor and Company of the Massachusetts Bay in New England*, edited by N.B. Shurtleff (Boston, MA: William White, 1853).

2. Why do the Quakers seem to pose such a threat to the moral climate of the colony, according to the Court? You may want to compare the passage concerning the Quakers with the Flushing citizens' petition for tolerance in Chapter 4.
3. Even though the selection focuses on the negative, what might be inferred from the document about the Court's notion of an ideal Puritan society?

Whereas the most wise & holy God, for several years past, hath not only warned us by his word, but chastized us with his rods, inflicting upon us many general (though lesser) judgments, but we have neither heard the word nor rod as we ought, so as to be effectually humbled for our sins to repent of them, reform, and amend our ways; hence it is the righteous God hath heightened our calamity, and given commission to the barbarous heathen to rise up against us, and to become a smart rod and severe scourge to us, in burning & depopulating several hopeful plantations, murdering many of our people of all sorts, and seeming as it were to cast us off, and putting us to shame, and not going forth with our armies, hereby speaking aloud to us to search and try our ways, and turn again unto the Lord our God, from whom we have departed with a great backsliding.

1. The Court, apprehending there is too great a neglect of discipline in the churches, and especially respecting those that are their children, through the non-acknowledgment of them according to the order of the gospel; in watching over them, as well as catechising of them, inquiring into their spiritual estates, that, being brought to take hold of the covenant, they may acknowledge & be acknowledged according to their relations to God & to his church, and their obligations to be the Lords, and to approve themselves so to be by a suitable profession & conversation; and do therefore solemnly recommend it unto the respective elders and brethren of the several churches through-

out this jurisdiction to take effectual course for reformation herein.

Hair and Clothes

2. Whereas there is manifest pride openly appearing amongst us in that long hair, like women's hair, is worn by some men, either their own or others hair made into periwigs, and by some women wearing borders of hair, and their cutting, curling, & immodest laying out their hair, which practice doeth prevail & increase, especially amongst the younger sort,—

This Court doeth declare against this ill custom as offensive to them, and divers sober Christians amongst us, and therefore do hereby exhort and advise all persons to use moderation in this respect; and further, do impower all grand juries to present to the County Court such persons, whither male or female, whom they shall judge to exceed in the premises; and the County Courts are hereby authorized to proceed against such delinquents either by admonition, fine, or correction, according to their good discretion.

3. Notwithstanding the wholesome laws already made by this Court for restraining excess in apparel, yet through corruption in many, and neglect of due execution of those laws, the evil of pride in apparel, both for costliness in the poorer sort, & vain, new, strange fashions, both in poor & rich, with naked breasts and arms, or, as it were, pinioned with the addition of superstitious ribbons both on hair & apparel; for redress whereof, it is ordered by this Court, that the County Courts, from time to time, do give strict charge to present all such persons as they shall judge to exceed in that kind, and if the grand jury shall neglect their duty herein, the County Court shall impose a fine upon them at their discretion.

And it is further ordered, that the County Court, single magistrate, Commissioners Court in Boston, have hereby power to summon all such persons so offending before them, and for the first offence to admonish them, and for each offence of that kind afterwards to impose a fine of ten shillings upon them, or, if unable to pay, to inflict such punishment as shall be by them thought most suitable to the nature of the offence; and the same judges above named are hereby impowered to judge of and execute the laws already extant against such excess.

Whereas it may be found amongst us, that men's thresholds are set up by God's thresholds, and man's posts besides God's posts, especially in the open meetings of Quakers, whose damnable heresies, abominable idolatrys, are hereby promoted, embraced, and practiced, to the scandal of religion, hazard of souls, and provocation of divine jealousy against this people, for prevention & reformation whereof, it is ordered by this Court and the authority thereof, that every person found at a Quakers meeting shall be apprehended, ex officio, by the constable, and by warrant from a magistrate or commissioner shall be committed to the house of correction, and there to have the discipline of the house applied to them, and to be kept to work, with bread & water, for three days, and then released, or else shall pay five pounds in money as a fine to the county for such offense; and all constables neglecting their duty in not faithfully executing this order shall incur the penalty of four pounds, upon conviction, one third whereof to the informer.

And touching the law of importation of Quakers, that it may be more strictly executed, and none transgressing to escape punishment,—

It is hereby ordered, that the penalty to that law averred be in no case abated to less than twenty pounds.

5. Whereas there is so much profanes amongst us in persons turning their backs upon the public worship before it be finished and the blessing pronounced,—

It is ordered by this Court, that the officers of the churches, or select-men, shall take care to prevent such disorders, by appointing persons to shut the meeting house doors, or any other meet way to attain the end.

Disorderly Youth

6. Whereas there is much disorder & rudeness in youth in many congregations in time of the worship of God, where-

by sin & profaness is greatly increased, for reformation whereof,—

It is ordered by this Court, that the select-men do appoint such place or places in the meeting house for children or youth to sit in where they may be most together and in public view, and that the officers of the churches, or select-men, do appoint some grave & sober person or persons to take a particular care of and inspection over them, who are hereby required to present a list of the names of such, who, by their own observance or the information of others, shall be found delinquent, to the next magistrate or Court, who are impowered for the first offence to admonish them, for the second offence to impose a fine of five shillings on their parents or governors, or order the children to be whipt, and if incorrigible, to be whipt with ten stripes, or sent to the house of correction for three days.

7. Whereas the name of God is profaned by common swearing and cursing in ordinary communication, which is a sin that grows amongst us, and many hear such oaths and curses, and conceals the same from authority, for reformation whereof, it is ordered by this Court, that the laws already in force against this sin be vigorously prosecuted; and, as addition thereunto, it is further ordered, that all such persons who shall at any time hear profane oaths and curses spoken by any person or persons, and shall neglect to disclose the same to some magistrate, commissioner, or constable, such persons shall incur the same penalty provided in that law against swearers.

8. Whereas the shameful and scandalous sin of excessive drinking, tipling, & company keeping in taverns, &c, ordinarys, grows upon us, for reformation whereof,—

It is commended to the care of the respective County Courts not to license any more public houses than are absolutely necessary in any town, and to take care that none be licensed but persons of approved sobriety and fidelity to law and good order; and that licensed houses be regulated in their improvement for the refreshing & entertainment of travailers & strangers only, and all town dwellers are hereby strictly enjoined & required to forbear spending their time or estates in such common houses of entertainment, to drink & tipple, upon penalty of five shillings for every offence, or, if poor, to be whipt, at the discretion of the judge, not exceeding five stripes; and every ordinary keeper, permitting persons to transgress as above said, shall incur the penalty of five shillings for each offence in that kind; and any magistrate, commissioner, or select-men are impowered & required vigorously to put the above-said law in execution.

And, further, it is ordered, that all private, unlicensed houses of entertainment be diligently searched out, and the penalty of this law strictly imposed; and that all such houses may be the better discovered, the select-men of every town shall choose some sober and discreet persons, to be authorized from the County Court, each of whom shall take the charge of ten or twelve families of his neighborhood, and shall diligently inspect them, and present the names of such persons so transgressing to the magistrate, commissioners, or select-men of the town, who shall return the same to be proceeded with by the next County Court as the law directs; and the persons so chosen and authorized, and attending their duty faithfully therein, shall have one third of the fines allowed them; but, if neglect of their duty, and shall be so judged by authority, they shall incur the same penalty provided against unlicensed houses.

Contempt of Authority

9. Whereas there is a woeful breach of the fifth commandment to be found amongst us, in contempt of authority civil, ecclesiastical, and domestical, this Court doeth declare, that sin is highly provoking to the Lord, against which he hath borne severe testimony in his word, especially in that remarkable judgments upon Chorah and his company, and therefore do strictly require & command all persons under this government to reform so great an evil, least God from heaven punish offenders herein by some remarkable judgments. And it is further ordered, that all

County Courts, magistrates, commissioners, select-men, and grand jurors, according to their several capacities, do take strict care that the laws already made & provided in this case be duly executed, and particularly that evil of inferiors absenting themselves out of the families whereunto they belong in the night, and meeting with corrupt company without leave, and against the mind & to the great grief of their superiors, which evil practice is of a very perilous nature, and the root of much disorder.

It is therefore ordered by this Court, that whatever inferior shall be legally convicted of such an evil practice, such persons shall be punished with admonition for the first offence, with fine not exceeding ten shillings, or whipping not exceeding five stripes, for all offenses of like nature afterwards.

10. Whereas the sin of idleness (which is a sin of Sodom) doeth greatly increase, notwithstanding the wholesome laws in force against the same, as an addition to that law,—

This Court doeth order, that the constable, with such other person or persons whom the select-men shall appoint, shall inspect particular families, and present a list of the names of all idle persons to the select-men, who are hereby strictly required to proceed with them as already the law directs, and in case of obstinacy, by charging the constable with them, who shall convey them to some magistrate, by him to be committed to the house of correction.

11. Whereas there is oppression in the midst of us, not only by such shopkeepers and merchants who set excessive prizes on their goods, also by mechanics but *also by mechanics* and day laborers, who are daily guilty of that evil, for redress whereof, & as an addition to the law, title Oppression, it is ordered by this Court, that any person that judgeth himself oppressed by shopkeepers or merchants in setting excessive prices on their goods, have hereby liberty to make their complaint to the grand jurors, or otherwise by petition to the County Court immediately, who shall send to the person accused, and if the Court, upon examination, judge the person complaining injured, they shall cause the

offender to return double the overplus, or more then the equal price, to the injured person, and also impose a fine on the offenders at the discretion of the Court; and if any person judge himself oppressed by mechanics or day laborers, they may make complaint thereof to the select-men of the town, who if upon the examination do find such complaint just, having respect to the quality of the pay, and the length or shortness of the day labor, they shall cause the offender to make double restitution to the party injured, and pay a fine of double the value exceeding the due price.

12. Whereas there is a loose & sinful custom of going or riding from town to town, and that oft times men & women together, upon pretense of going to lecture, but it appears to be merely to drink & revel in ordinarys & taverns, which is in itself scandalous, and it is to be feared a notable means to debauch our youth and hazard the chastity of such as are drawn forth thereunto, for prevention whereof,—

It is ordered by this Court, that all single persons who, merely for their pleasure, take such journeys, & frequent such ordinaryes, shall be reputed and accounted riotous & unsober persons, and of ill behavior, and shall be liable to be summoned to appear before any County Court, magistrate, or commissioner, & being thereof convicted, shall give bond & sufficient sureties for the good behavior in twenty pounds, and upon refusal so to do, shall be committed to prison for ten days, or pay a fine of forty shillings for each offence.

Immorality Cannot Be Curtailed by Stricter Laws

William Bradford

William Bradford (1590–1657) governed Plymouth Colony nearly thirty years, first elected in 1621 after the original governor died in the first, difficult months of the colony's existence. Bradford is also known for writing his history of the colony, *Of Plymouth Plantation, 1620–1647*, from which the following selection is taken. In the passage, Bradford argues against imposing harsher laws regulating morality in his colony, basing his reasoning on a blend of theological and quasi-psychological assumptions about vice and human nature. While it is important to keep in mind the fact that Bradford is by no means advocating tolerance of human foibles, his measured views of law and the human propensity to sin are markedly less strident and censorious than were commonly expressed by his Puritan brethren. Indeed, his insight about the causal relation between strict laws and the eruption of "wickedness" in the third paragraph is striking for its psychological acuity.

As you read, consider the following questions:
1. Discuss in detail Bradford's basic views about human nature, and their relation to his understanding of sinfulness.
2. Of the three main reasons Bradford puts forth for the apparent epidemic of sin in the colonies, which do you find most convincing? Why?
3. Examine Bradford's "stream" metaphor in the third paragraph. How does this "reason" differ from the other two in its focus and basic assumptions?

Excerpted from *Of Plymouth Plantation, 1620–1647*, by William Bradford, edited by Samuel Eliot Morison and Emily M. Beck (New York: Alfred A. Knopf, 1952).

Marvelous it may be to see and consider how some kind of wickedness did grow and break forth here, in a land where the same was so much witnessed against and so narrowly looked unto, and severely punished when it was known, as in no place more, or so much, that I have known or heard of; insomuch that they have been somewhat censured even by moderate and good men for their severity in punishments. And yet all this could not suppress the breaking out of sundry notorious sins (as this year [1642], besides other, gives us too many sad precedents and instances), especially drunkenness and uncleanness. Not only incontinency between persons unmarried, for which many both men and women have been punished sharply enough, but some married persons also. But that which is worse, even sodomy and buggery (things fearful to name) have broken forth in this land oftener than once.

I say it may justly be marveled at and cause us to fear and tremble at the consideration of our corrupt natures, which are so hardly bridled, subdued, and mortified; nay, cannot by any other means but the powerful work and grace of God's Spirit. But (besides this) one reason may be that the devil may carry a greater spite against the churches of Christ and the Gospel here, by how much the more they endeavor to preserve holiness and purity among them and strictly punish the contrary when it arises either in church or commonwealth; that he might cast a blemish and stain upon them in the eyes of [the] world, who use to be rash in judgment. I would rather think thus, than that Satan has more power in these heathen lands, as some have thought, than in more Christian nations, especially over God's servants in them.

Limits of Strict Laws
Another reason may be that it may be in this case as it is with waters when their streams are stopped or dammed up. When they get passage they flow with more violence and make more noise and disturbance than when they are suffered to run quietly in their own channels; so wickedness

being here more stopped by strict laws, and the same more nearly looked unto so as it cannot run in a common road of liberty as it would and is inclined, it searches everywhere and at last breaks out where it gets vent.

A third reason may be, here (as I am verily persuaded) is not more evils in this kind, nor nothing near so many by proportion as in other places; but they are here more discovered and seen and made public by due search, inquisition, and due punishment; for the churches look narrowly to their members, and the magistrates over all, more strictly than in other places. Besides, here the people are but few in comparison of other places which are full and populous and lie hid, as it were, in a wood or thicket and many horrible evils by that means are never seen nor known; whereas here they are, as it were, brought into the light and set in the plain field, or rather on a hill, made conspicuous to the view of all.

The Punishment of Sexual Misconduct

Plymouth Colony

Many readers are familiar with Nathaniel Hawthorne's classic novel *The Scarlet Letter,* in which heroine Hester Prynne is punished for adultery by being compelled to wear a stigmatizing red "A" on her gown. Although Hawthorne's nineteenth-century novel is set in Salem, the situation he envisioned for Hester was based on the actual laws and practices of colonial New England regarding sexual misbehavior. It is difficult to say authoritatively that the Puritans of New England were markedly more intolerant of sexual transgressions than other seventeenth-century European Christians; for example, criminal and even capital prosecutions of homosexual behavior continued throughout the Enlightenment and into the nineteenth century. However, the Puritans' near-obsession with regulating sexual matters was greatly the by-product of a religious worldview that at once valorized the ideal of Christian marriage (as opposed to the celibacy exalted by the Roman Catholic Church) and located God's judgment in even the most private of realms, whether the human conscience or the bedroom. Court documents indicate that the laws codified in the following selection from the Plymouth Colony Records (PCR) were indeed regularly enforced, along with the prescribed punishments.

As you read, consider the following questions:
1. Consider the various crimes and their respective punishments. How does the relative laxity or severity of the punishment indicate the Puritan hierarchy of social as well as moral values?

Excerpted from *Records of the Colony of New Plymouth in New England*, edited by Nathaniel Shurtleff and David Pulsifer (New York: AMS Press, 1968).

2. In what way are lying and disguise related to sexual misconduct in these records?
3. Compare the document to the Virginia General Assembly code of laws and note the similarities and differences in tone and language as well as content.

November 15, 1636: Capital offences liable to death. Sodomy, rapes, buggery. Adultery to be punished. (Offences criminal, Altered.) [Adultery crossed out] fornication and other unclean carriages to be punished at the discretion of the magistrates according to the nature thereof. Fornication before contract or marriage. (PCR 11:12)

Permission for Marriage

That none be allowed to marry that are under the covert of parents but by their consent and approbation. But in case consent cannot be had then it shall be with the consent of the governor, or some assistant to whom the persons are known whose care it shall be to see the marriage be fit before it be allowed by him. And after approbation be three several times published before the solemnising of it. Or else in places where there is no such meetings that contracts or agreements of marriage may be so published, that then it shall be lawful to publish them by a writing thereof made and set upon the usual public place for the space of fifteen days. Provided that the writing be under some magistrate's hand or by his order. (PCR 11:13)

December 4, 1638: Whereas diverse persons unfit for marriage both in regard of their young years as also in regard of their weak estate, some practicing the inveigling of men's daughters and maids under guardians (contrary to their parents and guardians liking) and of maid servants without leave and liking of their masters, it is therefore enacted by the Court that if any shall make any motion of marriage to any man's daughter or maid servant not having first obtained leave and consent of the parents or master so to do shall be punished either by fine or corporal punishment or both, at the discretion of the bench and according to the nature of the offence.

It is also enacted that if a motion of marriage be duly made to the master and through any sinister end or covetous desire he will not consent thereunto, then the cause to be made known unto the magistrates and they to set down

The Puritans strongly believed in the sanctity of marriage and harshly punished sexual misconduct by both men and women.

such order therein as upon examination of the case shall appear to be most equal on both parts. (PCR 11:29)

Premarital Sex

June 4, 1645: It is enacted et cetera that every person or persons which shall commit carnal copulation before or without lawful contract shall be punished whether with corporal punishment by whipping or else pay ten pounds a piece fine and be imprisoned during the pleasure of the Court so it be not above three days, but if they be or will be married one to another, then but ten pounds both and imprisonment as aforesaid. And by a lawful contract the Court understands the mutual consent of two parties with the consent of parents or guardians (if there be any to be had) and a solemn promise of marriage in due time to each other before two competent witnesses. And if any person or persons shall commit carnal copulation after contract and before marriage shall both pay five pounds and be both imprisoned during the pleasure of the Court so it be not above three days, or else in case they cannot or will not pay the fine then to suffer corporal punishment by whipping. (PCR 11:46)

Disguise and Dishonesty

Whereas some abuses have formerly broken out amongst us by disguising wearing visors and strange apparel to lacivious ends and purposes It is therefore enacted, that if any person or persons shall hereafter use any such disguisements visors strange apparel or the like to such lacivious and evil ends and intents, and be thereof convict by due course of law shall pay fifty shillings for the first offence or else be publicly whipt and for the second time five pounds or be publicly whipt and be bound to the behavior if the Bench shall see cause. (PCR 11:48)

June 9, 1653: That every person of the age of discretion which is accounted sixteen years who shall wittingly and willingly make or publish any lie which may be pernicious to the public weal or tending to the damage or hurt of any particular person or with intent to deceive and abuse the people with false news or reports and the same duly proved before any one magistrate who hath hereby power granted to hear and determine all offences against this law; shall be fined for every such default ten shillings; And if the party be unable to pay then to be set in the stocks so long as the said magistrate shall appoint in some open place not exceeding the space of two hours. (PCR 11:63)

Adultery and "Uncleanness"

September 29, 1658: It is enacted by the court and the authority thereof that whosoever shall commit adultery shall be severely punished by whipping two several times; namely once whiles the Court is in being at which they are convicted of the fact and the 2cond time as the Court shall order and likewise to wear two capital letters namely A D cut out in cloth and sowed on their uppermost garments on their arm or back; and if at any time they shall be taken without the said letters whiles they are in the government so worn to be forth with taken and publicly whipt. (PCR 11:95)

July 2, 1667: It is enacted by the Court that such as commit fornication or common drunkards that no fine be received from them for their fact until they have been convicted thereof before the Court unless some unavoidable impediment shall hinder their appearance thereat. (PCR 11:219)

June 1670: It is enacted by the Court that whosoever having committed uncleanness in another colony and shall come hither and have not satisfied the law where the fact was committed they shall be sent back or here punished according to the nature of the crime as if the act had been here done. (PCR 11:229)

A Proposal to Unite the Colonies

William Penn

Quaker, pacifist, and progressive, William Penn nonetheless had military protection in mind when he wrote what is regarded as the first proposal for a colonial union in 1697. As founder of Pennsylvania, a colony known for its tolerance of dissidents and free thinkers, Penn was something of a utopian visionary. But as the eighteenth century neared, even Penn was faced with the realities born of the recent, bloody conflict with the Native Americans during King Philip's War (1675–1676). His 1697 plan for a union had pragmatic aims in mind, recognizing the common interests all the English crown colonies shared about peace and security. Amid the French and Indian War (1754–1763) a similar proposal for union was put forth, at the Albany conference, by Benjamin Franklin; like Penn's, it was entertained but ultimately rejected. Yet Penn's plan is commonly regarded as the model for the U.S. Constitution, significant for its pointed omission of religious and moral matters as within the province of government.

As you read, consider the following questions:

1. Compare and contrast the governmental structure that Penn envisions with that put forth by the Virginia General Assembly. Which seems a surer guarantee of representative government?
2. Penn proposes that the representatives be chosen based on "sense, sobriety, and substance." What may he mean by those qualities? What is the effect of Penn not specifying definitions of the three traits?

Excerpted from *Penn's Plan of Union*, by William Penn (Pennsylvania, 1697).

3. What may be inferred about Penn's attitude toward royal authority? How does it differ from that suggested in other colonial legal documents?

A brief and plain scheme how the English colonies in the North parts of America,—viz., Boston, Connecticut, Rhode Island, New York, New Jersey, Pennsylvania, Maryland, Virginia, and Carolina,—may be made more useful to the crown and one another's peace and safety with an universal concurrence.

1. That the several colonies before mentioned do meet once a year, and oftener if need be during the war, and at least once in two years in times of peace, by their stated and appointed deputies, to debate and resolve of such measures as are most advisable for their better understanding and the public tranquility and safety.

2. That, in order to it, two persons, well qualified for sense, sobriety, and substance, be appointed by each province as their representatives or deputies, which in the whole make the congress to consist of twenty persons.

3. That the king's commissioner, for that purpose specially appointed, shall have the chair and preside in the said congress.

4. That they shall meet as near as conveniently may be to the most central colony for ease of the deputies.

5. Since that may in all probability be New York, both because it is near the center of the colonies and for that it is a frontier and in the king's nomination, the governor of that colony may therefore also be the king's high commissioner during the session, after the manner of Scotland.

6. That their business shall be to hear and adjust all matters of complaint or difference between province and province. As, 1st, where persons quit their own province and go to another, that they may avoid their just debts, though they be able to pay them; 2nd, where offenders fly justice, or justice cannot well be had upon such offenders in the provinces that entertain them; 3rd, to prevent or cure

injuries in point of commerce; 4th, to consider the ways and means to support the union and safety of these provinces against the public enemies. In which congress the quotas of men and charges will be much easier and more equally set than it is possible for any establishment made here to do; for the provinces, knowing their own condition and one another's, can debate that matter with more freedom and satisfaction, and better adjust and balance their affairs in all respects for their common safety.

7. That, in times of war, the king's high commissioner shall be general or chief commander of the several quotas upon service against the common enemy, as he shall be advised, for the good and benefit of the whole.

CHRONOLOGY

1492
Italian sea captain Christopher Columbus arrives in the Caribbean.

1497
Venetian-born explorer John Cabot claims Labrador, New-foundland, and the New England coast for King Henry VII of England. 1513 Spain's Ponce de León arrives in Florida.

1517
Martin Luther posts his ninety-five theses on the door of Wittenberg Cathedral detailing his reasons for rejecting the Catholic Church and beginning the Protestant Reformation.

1529
King Henry VIII breaks England's ties with the Catholic Church over the pope's refusal to grant him a divorce from his Spanish wife.

1533
John Calvin declares himself a Protestant.

1536
Calvin publishes his *Institutes of the Christian Religion*.

1539
Hernando de Soto and six thousand men explore the region that will become the southwestern United States.

1553
Mary Tudor, daughter of Henry VIII, ascends the throne of England and returns England to Roman Catholicism; Protestant reformers begin to flee to Europe.

1558

Elizabeth I becomes queen of England; Protestant exiles begin to return to England.

1563

The English government approves the Thirty-nine Articles, instituting some Protestant reforms but disappointing extremists who want to eliminate every vestige of Romanism from the Church of England.

1585

More than one hundred colonists establish the first Roanoke colony off the coast of present-day North Carolina.

1590

A supply ship returning to Roanoke three years after the last visit discovers the original colony has been ransacked and abandoned, leaving no trace of the settlers left behind.

1603

James I, the first of the Stuart monarchy, becomes king of England and quickly antagonizes the Puritans by asserting the divine right of kings.

1606

The English receive permission from King James I to establish colonies in the New World.

1607

John Smith and company found Jamestown, Virginia; a group of English Puritans known as Separatists arrives in Amsterdam and eventually settles in Leyden in 1609.

1608

English navigator Henry Hudson explores the Chesapeake and Delaware Bays and the Hudson River.

1612

John Rolfe harvests the first successful tobacco crop in Virginia.

1619

The Virginia House of Burgesses, the first elected legislature in the colonies, meets for the first time; a Dutch ship brings the first African slaves to Jamestown.

1620

The first permanent settlement of English Puritans in New England is established at Plymouth by Separatists who draft the Mayflower Compact; they will come to be known as the pilgrims.

1621

William Bradford is chosen as governor of Plymouth Plantation, and though he is never able to secure a royal charter for his pilgrim community, he will govern successfully for a number of years without great interference from London.

1623

English traders and fishermen establish settlements in New Hampshire.

1624

Dutch colonists arrive in New York and New Jersey; England's King James I takes control of the Virginia Colony and makes it a royal settlement.

1625

Charles I becomes king of England; his contempt for Parliament and assertion of monarchical authority as well as his apparent opposition to Puritan practices dismays Puritans.

1628

A charter is granted by the Council of New England to a group of Puritan merchants organized as the New England Company.

1629

The New England Company reorganizes and receives a royal charter as the Massachusetts Bay Company; John Winthrop is selected by a "general vote and full consent" as the first governor of the colony.

1630

Winthrop's group of Puritans, one thousand strong, establish the Massachusetts Bay Colony.

1631

Roger Williams arrives in New England and is welcomed there because of his reputation as an eloquent preacher.

1634

The second Lord Baltimore founds Maryland.

1635

Thomas Hooker and sixty followers found Hartford, the first permanent settlement in Connecticut; the Reverend Richard Mather arrives in Massachusetts and begins a long line of Puritan ministers in the Mather family, including son Increase Mather and grandson Cotton Mather.

1636

Williams is banished from the Massachusetts Bay Colony and founds Providence, Rhode Island; Harvard College, the first American college, is founded.

1637

Anne Hutchinson is put on trial for heresy; the trial results in her conviction and banishment; war breaks out between English settlers in the Connecticut Valley and the Pequot Indians; it ends with the virtual decimation of the Pequot tribe.

1641

The calling of the Long Parliament brings Puritans into control of the English government; the Body of Liberties is drafted and defines basic liberties for the Massachusetts Bay Colony.

1642

The English civil war begins between the Cavaliers (supporters of the king) and the Roundheads (supporters of Parliament, who were largely Puritan); Puritan migration to America slows to a trickle.

1644

Roger Williams establishes the colony of Rhode Island with full freedom of worship for all faiths and no mandatory taxation in support of any religion.

1646

The General Court passes a law requiring everyone within a Puritan town to attend church services; religious heresy is made punishable by death.

1649

The Roundheads defeat the Cavaliers; Charles I is captured and beheaded.

1656

The first Quakers arrive in Massachusetts, where they are arrested and banished.

1660

The Restoration begins in England; Puritan rule ends as Charles II ascends the throne; some English Puritan leaders migrate to New England.

1670

English settlers found Charles Town in Carolina.

1675–1676

King Philip's War rages across New England as various Puritan towns come under attack from Indians and Boston is threatened before the Wampanoags are defeated and their leader Metacomet (King Philip) is killed.

1682

William Penn founds Philadelphia, Pennsylvania.

1683

Massachusetts's 1629 colonial charter is abolished, leaving the colonial government with no legal authority.

1686

The Dominion of New England is created in London by James II to bring all of New England under a single royal governor, thereby eliminating the existing colonial assemblies.

1688

The Glorious Revolution takes place in England; William and Mary become joint sovereigns and the Catholic king, James II, flees to France; New Englanders, upon hearing of events in England, gather in a mob and drive Edward Andros, the governor appointed by James II, from office; Andros is eventually imprisoned; the colonies regain former separate and legal status, except for Massachusetts, which remains without a charter.

1691

William and Mary grant Massachusetts a new charter; it restores some power to the General Court and incorporates the Plymouth Colony within Massachusetts; it provides for a royal governor appointed by the Crown, however, and many of the colonies' former rights and liberties are lost.

1692
Nineteen residents of Salem, Massachusetts, are executed for witchcraft in the largest single episode of its kind in New England; several accusers will eventually recant.

1701
Yale University is founded in New Haven, Connecticut.

1713
Carolina is divided into two colonies: North Carolina and South Carolina.

1733
James Edward Oglethorpe founds Savannah, Georgia.

1734
Jonathan Edwards, a preeminent Puritan preacher, begins a series of influential sermons fusing rationalism and mysticism, initiating the Great Awakening in New England.

1754
The French and Indian Wars begin over disputed land in the Ohio River Valley; the wars will last nine years, ending in 1763 with the Treaty of Paris.

1764
In response to the Sugar Act, the Currency Act, and other tariffs, Boston lawyer James Otis decries taxation without representation at a town hall meeting.

1765
Parliament passes the wide-ranging Stamp Act, which requires colonists to pay taxes directly to England; pressure by colonial outrage, protests, and riots forces the law's repeal a year later.

1767

The Townshend Acts impose a new series of tariffs on the colonies, provoking more boycotts, riots, and protests.

1770

A confrontation between British soldiers and a mob of citizens results in the Boston Massacre and the deaths of five colonists and the injury of six others; later the same year, most of the soldiers involved are acquitted of culpability.

1773

The Tea Act grants a monopoly to London's East India Company; in protest, a group of colonists disguised as Mohawk Indians raid three merchant ships in Boston Harbor and dump 342 bins of tea into the water.

1774

In angry response to the colonists' actions, Parliament enacts a series of punitive measures known as the Coercive or Intolerable Acts.

1775

The first shots of the American Revolution are fired in Massachusetts; George Washington assumes control of the Continental forces.

1776

Congress approves the Declaration of Independence.

FOR FURTHER RESEARCH

Melinda Allman, ed., *The Thirteen Colonies: Primary Sources*. San Diego: Lucent Books, 2002.

Bernard Bailyn, *The New England Merchants in the Seventeenth Century*. Cambridge, MA: Harvard University Press, 1955.

Emory Battis, *Saints and Sectarians*. Chapel Hill: University of North Carolina Press, 1962.

Paul Boyer and Stephen Nissenbaum, *Salem Possessed*. Cambridge, MA: Harvard University Press, 1974.

William Bradford, *Of Plymouth Plantation, 1620–1647*. Ed. Samuel Eliot Morison. New York: Alfred A. Knopf, 1959.

Carl Bridenbaugh, *Cities in the Wilderness*. New York: Ronald, 1938.

Samuel Brockunier, *The Irrepressible Democrat*. New York: Ronald, 1940.

J.M. Bumstead, ed., *The Great Awakening: The Beginnings of Evangelical Pietism in America*. Waltham, MA: Blaisdell Ginn, 1970.

George Lincoln Burr, ed., *Narratives of the Witchcraft Cases, 1648–1706*. New York: Barnes & Noble, 1914.

Bruce Catton and William B. Catton, *The Bold and Magnificent Dream: America's Founding Years, 1492–1815*. Garden City, NY: Doubleday, 1978.

David Colbert, ed., *Eyewitness to America*. New York: Pantheon Books, 1997.

Patrick Collinson, *The Elizabethan Puritan Movement*. Berkeley and Los Angeles: University of California Press, 1967.

Andrew Delbanco, *The Puritan Ordeal*. Cambridge, MA: Harvard University Press, 1989.

Richard Dunn, *Puritans and Yankees*. New York: Norton, 1971.

Emory Elliott, ed., *American Literature: A Prentice-Hall Anthology*. Englewood Cliffs, NJ: Prentice-Hall, 1991.

Charles George and Kathleen George, *The Protestant Mind of the English Reformation*. Princeton, NJ: Princeton University Press, 1961.

C.C. Goen, ed., *The Works of Jonathan Edwards: The Great Awakening*. New Haven, CT: Yale University Press, 1972.

Stephen Greenblatt, *Shakespearean Negotiations*. Berkeley and Los Angeles: University of California Press, 1988.

Giles Gunn, ed., *Early American Writing*. New York: Penguin Books, 1994.

Richard Hakluyt, *Principle Navigations, Voyages of the English Nation*. Vol. 3. London: n.p., 1600.

John Hammond, *Leah and Rachel, or, the Two Fruitful Sisters Virginia and Maryland: Their Present Condition, Impartially Stated and Related*. N.p., 1656.

Thomas Hariot, *A Brief and True Report of the New Found Land of Virginia Directed to the Investors, Farmers, and Well-Wishers of the Project of Colonizing and Planting There*. London: n.p., 1588.

David Hawke, ed., *U.S. Colonial History: Readings and Documents*. New York: Bobbs-Merrill, 1966.

Alan Heimert, *Religion and the American Mind*. Cambridge, MA: Harvard University Press, 1966.

Christopher Hill, *Society and Puritanism in Pre-Revolutionary England*. New York: Oxford University Press, 1967.

Francis Jennings, *The Invasion of America*. Chapel Hill: University of North Carolina Press, 1975.

Karen Ordahl Kupperman, ed., *Major Problems in American Colonial History*. Lexington, MA: D.C. Heath, 1993.

George Langdon, *Pilgrim Colony*. New Haven, CT: Yale University Press, 1966.

Douglas Leach, *Flintlock and Tomahawk: New England in King Philip's War*. New York: Macmillan, 1958.

David Levin, ed., *What Happened in Salem?* New York: Twayne, 1950.

David S. Lovejoy, *The Glorious Revolution in America*. New York: Harper and Row, 1972.

Michael McGiffert, ed., *Puritanism and the American Experience*. Reading, MA: Addison-Wesley, 1969.

Gottlieb Mittelberger, *Journey to Pennsylvania in the Year 1750*. Trans. Carl T. Eben. Philadelphia: John Joseph McVey, 1898.

Edmund S. Morgan, ed., *The Founding of Massachusetts: Historians and Their Sources*. Indianapolis: Bobbs-Merrill, 1964.

Samuel Eliot Morison, *Builders of the Bay Colony*. Boston: Houghton Mifflin, 1930.

Thomas Morton, *A New English Canaan*. Vol. 4, 1637. Reprint, Boston: n.p., 1883.

D.M. Palliser, *The Age of Elizabeth, 1547–1603*. Essex, UK: Longman, 1983.

Records of Salem Witchcraft. Roxbury, MA: W. Elliot Woodward, 1864.

Mary Rowlandson, *A True History of the Captivity and Restoration of Mrs. Mary Rowlandson, a Minister's Wife in New-England*. London: Joseph Poole, 1682.

Darrett B. Rutman, *Winthrop's Boston*. Chapel Hill: University of North Carolina Press, 1965.

Neal Salisbury, *Manitou and Providence: Indians, Europeans, and the Making of New England*. New York: Oxford University Press, 1982.

Charles M. Segal and David C. Stinebeck, *Puritans, Indians, and Manifest Destiny*. New York: G.P. Putnam's Sons, 1977.

Kenneth Silverman, *The Life and Times of Cotton Mather*. New York: Harper and Row, 1984.

Richard Slotkin and James K. Folsom, eds., *So Dreadful a Judgment: Puritan Responses to King Philip's War, 1676–1677*. Middletown, CT: Wesleyan University Press, 1978.

Lacey Baldwin Smith, *The Elizabethan World*. Boston: Houghton Mifflin, 1991.

Marion L. Starkey, *The Devil in Massachusetts: A Modern Inquiry into the Salem Witch Trials*. New York: Alfred A. Knopf, 1949.

T.J. Stiles, ed., *In Their Own Words: The Colonizers*. New York: Berkeley, 1998.

Alden T. Vaughan and Edward W. Clark, eds., *Puritans Among the Indians*. Cambridge, MA: Belknap Press of Harvard University Press, 1981.

Richard Walsh, ed., *The Mind and Spirit of Early America: Sources in American History, 1607–1789*. New York: Meredith, 1969.

Michael Walzer, *The Revolution of the Saints*. Cambridge, MA: Harvard University Press, 1965.

Francois Wendel, *Calvin: The Origins and Development of His Religious Thought*. London: Collins, 1963.

William Wood, *New England's Prospect: A True, Lively, and Experimental Description of That Part of America, Commonly Called New England*. London: John Dawson, 1639.

Howard Zinn, *A People's History of the United States, 1492–Present*. New York: HarperCollins, 1995.

INDEX

will toward, 92–93
Native Americans are
advantageous to, 93
Native Americans desiring
peace with, 79
proposal to unite,
202–203
see also Jamestown
colony; law(s); Roanoke
Island
Cooke, Abraham, 45, 46,
49
copper, 37–38
Cotton, John, 139
Cromwell, Oliver, 18, 137

Dare, Virginia, 44
de Soto, Hernando, 13
Discovery (ship), 53
disease, 66, 85–86
Drake, Sir Francis, 35, 41

Easty, Mary, 130–35
education, 22–23
Edwards, Jonathan,
165–66
Elizabeth I (queen of
England), 16, 32, 53
England
colonial conflict with,
26–28
Enlightenment and, 25–26
expeditions from, 32–33
first colonies from, 12–14
religion and, 16–18
tobacco trade with
colonies, 14–15
Enlightenment, 24–26

explorers, 13
John Cabot, 32
London Company, 33
Sir Walter Raleigh, 32–33

Flushing Remonstrance,
161–62
Franklin, Benjamin, 23
French and Indian Wars
(1754–1763), 27

Gilbert, Sir Humphrey, 34
Godspeed (ship), 53
Good, Sarah, 130
government
Native American, 70
see also law(s)
Great Awakening, 24–25,
137–38
Grenville, Sir Richard, 13,
34

Hakluyt, Richard, 13, 44
Hammond, John, 103
Hance (the Surgeon), 47
Hariot, Thomas, 68
Hart, Edward, 161
Harvard University, 23
Henry VII (king of
England), 32
Henry VIII (king of
England), 16
Hobbes, Thomas, 25
humans
God does not owe
redemption to, 172–73
God's vengeance and
wrath on, 166–69,

187–88
church/state separation
and, 179
on contempt of authority,
190–91
on dishonesty, 199–200
for disorderly youth,
188–89
against excess, 183–84
on gambling, 183–84
on hair and clothing, 187
on idleness, 183–84, 191
limits of strict, 194–95
on marriage, 197–99
for merchants and
shopkeepers, 191–92
on premarital sex, 199
punishment for
disobeying, 187–88
runaway slave, 24
self-government and,
179–80
should not interfere with
religious conscience,
151–52
on swearing and cursing,
189
on taverns, 189–90
on travel for pleasure, 192
León, Ponce de, 13
liberty of conscience,
158–60
London Company, 14, 33

Mangoak, 37–38
Manteo (Croatoan Indian),
44, 50
marriage, 22

for indentured servants,
107–108, 114–15
permission for, 197–99
Mary Tudor (queen of
England), 16
Massachusetts Bay Colony,
17, 22, 102
Massachusetts charter, 102
Massachusetts General
Court, 185
Massasoit (chief of the
Wampanoag), 33, 59, 61,
67
Mather, Cotton, 122
Mather, Increase, 20
Matoaka. See Pocahontas
Mayflower (ship), 17
Metacom, 94
Metacomet, 67
Mittelberger, Gottlieb, 109
Morarok, 37
Morton, Thomas, 80

Narragansett, 94
Native Americans
admiration of colonists,
73
advantageous friendship
with the colonists, 93
attacks by, 94, 95–97
awe and fear of the
colonists, 75–77
on the Bible, 73–74
burning of the country, 87
capturing colonists, 97–99
clothing, 69
colonial attitudes toward,
66

length of colony on, 35
Native Americans on,
39–40, 69–77
pearls on, 36–37
return journey to, 44,
45–47
carved letters found at
abandoned site during,
48–49
chests found at site of
during, 49–50
return voyage from,
50–52
return to England from,
41–43
Rolfe, John, 14, 15
Roman Catholic Church,
137
Rousseau, Jean-Jacques, 25
Rowlandson, Mary, 67,
94–95
runaway slave laws, 24

Salem Court, 130
Salem Town, 20, 102
Salem Village, 20, 102
Salem witch trials, 20–21,
101–102, 130–35
Separatists, 17
sex, premarital, 199
Skinner, Ralph, 47
slavery, 21–22, 24, 116
reasons for Quaker
opposition to, 118–21
as un-Christian, 117–18
smallpox, 66
Smith, John, 15
Smith, Lacey Baldwin, 13

Sons of Liberty, 28
Spicer, Edward, 45, 46, 47
Squanto, 59
Stone, Lawrence, 18
Stuyvesant, Peter, 161
Susan Constant (ship), 53

tariff acts, 28
taxation without
representation, 28
Thanksgiving celebration,
18, 33, 60–61
Tituba, 20–21, 101, 130
tobacco farming, 14–15,
33, 101
trade
among Native Americans,
83
tobacco, 14–15
Tuscarora Indian War
(1711–1713), 24

universities, 23

Virginia. *See* Jamestown
colony
Virginia General Assembly,
181

Wampanoag, 33, 67, 94
Wampanoag war, 185
Ward, Nathaniel, 156
Wheelwright, John, 139
White, John, 34, 44
William and Mary College,
23
William III (king of
England), 102